LARGE-SCALE
ASSESSMENT

EXPERTS IN ASSESSMENT

SERIES EDITORS
THOMAS R. GUSKEY AND ROBERT J. MARZANO

JUDITH ARTER, JAY MCTIGHE
SCORING RUBRICS IN THE CLASSROOM: USING PERFORMANCE CRITERIA FOR ASSESSING AND IMPROVING STUDENT PERFORMANCE

JANE M. BAILEY, THOMAS R. GUSKEY
IMPLEMENTING STUDENT-LED CONFERENCES

THOMAS R. GUSKEY, JANE M. BAILEY
DEVELOPING GRADING AND REPORTING SYSTEMS FOR STUDENT LEARNING

EDWARD KIFER
LARGE-SCALE ASSESSMENT: DIMENSIONS, DILEMMAS, AND POLICY

ROBERT J. MARZANO
DESIGNING A NEW TAXONOMY OF EDUCATIONAL OBJECTIVES

JAMES H. MCMILLAN
ESSENTIAL ASSESSMENT CONCEPTS FOR TEACHERS AND ADMINISTRATORS

JEFFREY K. SMITH, LISA F. SMITH, RICHARD DE LISI
NATURAL CLASSROOM ASSESSMENT: DESIGNING SEAMLESS INSTRUCTION AND ASSESSMENT

ISBN 0-7619-7756-2 (7-BOOK PAPER EDITION)
ISBN 0-7619-7757-0 (7-BOOK LIBRARY EDITION)

LARGE-SCALE ASSESSMENT

DIMENSIONS, DILEMMAS, AND POLICY

EDWARD KIFER

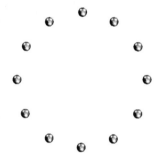

EXPERTS IN ASSESSMENT

SERIES EDITORS
THOMAS R. GUSKEY AND ROBERT J. MARZANO

CORWIN PRESS, INC.
A Sage Publications Company
Thousand Oaks, California

For information:

Corwin Press, Inc.
A Sage Publications Company
2455 Teller Road
Thousand Oaks, California 91320
E-mail: order@corwinpress.com

Sage Publications Ltd.
6 Bonhill Street
London EC2A 4PU
United Kingdom

Sage Publications India Pvt. Ltd.
M-32 Market
Greater Kailash I
New Delhi 110 048 India

Printed in the United States of America

Library of Congress Cataloging-in-Publication Data

Kifer, Edward.
    Large-scale assessment: Dimensions, dilemmas, and policy / by Edward Kifer.
        p.   cm. — (Experts in assessment kit)
Includes bibliographical references and index.
    ISBN 0-8039-6833-7 (cloth: alk. paper)
    ISBN 0-8039-6834-5 (pbk: alk. paper)
1. Educational tests and measurements. 2. Academic
achievement—Evaluation. 3. Educational evaluation—planning.
I. Title.   II. Series.
    LB3051 .K45 2000
    371.26—dc21   00-008163

This book is printed on acid-free paper.

01   02   03   04   05   10   9   8   7   6   5   4   3   2   1

Corwin Editorial Assistant: Catherine Kantor
Production Editor: Nevair Kabakian
Editorial Assistant: Victoria Cheng
Typesetter/Designer: Rebecca Evans
Cover Designer: Tracy E. Miller

Contents

Series Editors' Introduction

Standards, assessment, accountability, and grading—these are the issues that dominated discussions of education in the 1990s. Today, they are at the center of every modern education reform effort. As educators turn to the task of implementing these reforms, they face a complex array of questions and concerns that little in their background or previous experience has prepared them to address. This series is designed to help in that challenging task.

In selecting the authors, we went to individuals recognized as true experts in the field. The ideas of these scholar-practitioners have already helped shape current discussions of standards, assessment, accountability, and grading. But equally important, their work reflects a deep understanding of the complexities involved in implementation. As they developed their books for this series, we asked them to extend their thinking, to push the edge, and to present new perspectives on what should be done and how to do it. That is precisely what they did. The books they crafted provide not only cutting-edge perspectives but also practical guidelines for successful implementation.

We have several goals for this series. First, that it be used by teachers, school leaders, policy makers, government officials, and all those concerned with these crucial aspects of education reform. Second, that it helps broaden understanding of the complex issues involved in standards, assessment, accountability, and grading. Third, that it leads to more thoughtful policies and programs. Fourth, and most important, that it helps accomplish the basic goal for which all reform initiatives are intended—namely, to enable all students to learn excellently and to gain the many positive benefits of that success.

— *Thomas R. Guskey*
Robert J. Marzano
Series Editors

Preface

To say that assessments of student performance are more prevalent today than at any other period in our history is to state the obvious. Now, almost all states have some form of assessment as compared with 25 years ago when such testing was, with a few notable exceptions, either nonexistent or in its infancy. This growth is in addition to both more and more frequent national and international assessments and increased use of such college admission and placement tests such as the Scholastic Achievement Test and the American College Testing Program.

If these additional state, national, and international assessments were cut from the same cloth—merely mimicked the New York State Regents Examinations, for instance—their results would be reasonably easy to understand. There would be a history of their use, well-recognized and understood methods to create them, and well-defined educational contexts that produced them. What we have instead is a plethora of new assessments with varied purposes, short histories, and ill-defined contexts.

A striking example of what I mean is the so-called standards-based assessments. There is a naive consensus that standards-based assessments are "good things" despite perhaps their slight failings technically, and there are general perceptions that the higher the standards the better the assessments. It is, of course, difficult to argue against standards and even more difficult to be against high standards. Perceptions rule the day.

Yet, there are serious technical, conceptual, and pragmatic issues surrounding standards-based assessments. Although it is generally acknowledged that standard setting is an arbitrary process, not much is known about when high standards are too high or low standards are too low. How high is high enough? And high enough for what? When accountability systems for students or schools are based on standards-based assessments, we do not know much about how well students or schools are properly classified and what the implications are of the classification decisions. What are the educational implications of such decisions? Why is it, for example, that poor and minority students are more likely to fail to meet the standards than are wealthy and majority students?

I think it is important to raise issues about these and other such matters in this new assessment climate. To do so, I thought it desirable to give first a general, noncontroversial base for describing contemporary assessments. Hence, I developed what I call the assessment grid.

The grid contains 11 dimensions on which assessments may vary. Within the dimensions are features of the assessment about which decisions must be made and policies adopted. The grid, when used like a report card, provides, I believe, both a good way to describe an assessment and a way, based on their descriptions, to compare different assessments.

The grid and examples of its use on three large-scale assessments forms the first third of the book. I use the National Assessment of Educational Progress (NAEP), the International Association for the Evaluation of Educational Achievement (IEA) Third International Mathematics and Science Study (TIMSS), and the Kentucky Instructional Results Information System (KIRIS) to show how the report card might be used.

The second third of the book explicates the dimensions and facets of the grid. For each facet I raise issues that should be addressed when planning or understanding an assessment. In this section, I am mainly as nonjudgmental as I am capable of being.

The final third of the book contains what for me are big issues related to assessments and some conjectures about what should be done if one desires to see assessment results that reflect improvements in schools. I hope these opinions are controversial. My views on these issues across the board are, of course, the correct ones.

People tell me that I should be writing for an audience. I often wonder how many persons are really interested in assessments. I know quite a number of persons with technical interests whose work is innovative and who have done much to improve the technical qualities of the assessments I speak about. This book is not directly aimed at them because I have tried to minimize the technical talk. (One would hope they would be interested, however, in what their techniques have given birth to.) There are the tough-minded. They want to know whether scores are up or down, and they do not want to know the details. This book is not aimed at them, either. Although the devil is in the details, understanding them provides, I hope, a broader appreciation of the assessment arena. So, I guess that is my audience. It is those persons who are interested or affected by assessments who wish to think more about them and their influence. I hope, too, that those who are designing assessments might find this a useful source.

I enjoyed working on this book. As I wrote, I thought of colleagues I learned from and persons whose views have informed mine. Rather than mention some at the risk of forgetting one, I will only say that if you know me well enough to know my preference in wine, in all likelihood, I owe you.

I hope my first audience, Suzi, Martin, Chelle, and Kris, can wade through this and even smile at times.

— Edward Kifer

About the Author

Edward "Skip" Kifer received his PhD from the University of Chicago and the Measurement, Evaluation, and Statistical Analysis (MESA) specialization. At Chicago he was a resource colleague with the Ford Foundation Teacher Training Program, a member of the college admissions staff, and a statistical consultant to the Department of Education at the University of Chicago. He joined the faculty of the University of Kentucky in 1972. During his tenure at Kentucky, he has been a Spencer Foundation Fellow at the University of Stockholm and a visiting professor at both the State University of New York at Buffalo and the University of California, Los Angeles. Recently, he was the American Educational Research Association's Senior Research Fellow at the National Center for Education Statistics.

Skip teaches educational statistics and evaluation. His research interests are testing, assessment, and evaluation. He has conducted numerous evaluations and has written articles related to assessments and their consequences. Other arenas in which he has written include reviewing tests, attitude measurement, and construction of attitude measures. He played a major role in designing, implementing, and reporting the results of the Second International Mathematics Study. He was also one of five persons who planned the Commonwealth of Kentucky's assessment system and has served on both its national technical committee and a technical committee that oversees international evaluation studies.

While serving as an AERA Senior Research Fellow, he looked closely at the National Assessment of Educational Progress (NAEP) assessments and was particularly interested in questions of how those assessments might be linked to state assessments and vice versa. He is currently a member of NAEP's Design and Analysis Committee and continues to look for ways that NAEP results can inform other kinds of assessment results

CORWIN
PRESS

The Corwin Press logo—a raven striding across an open book—represents the happy union of courage and learning. We are a professional-level publisher of books and journals for K–12 educators, and we are committed to creating and providing resources that embody these qualities. Corwin's motto is "Success for All Learners."

CHAPTER 1

The Setting

The Status of Large-Scale Assessments

Large-scale assessments flourished during the decade of the 1990s. They were executed in varied contexts and focused on different academic content areas. Those who were interested could peruse results from scores of countries, multiple U.S. national assessments, and assessments from almost every U.S. state.[1] There was information about traditional content areas (e.g., mathematics, science) and more contemporary areas such as computers in education.

As the number and types of assessments increased, so too did the issues they addressed and, concomitantly, the issues they raised. This is especially the case because a major impetus for the plethora of assessments was the popularity of school reform efforts. Fueled, I believe, by *A Nation at Risk: The Imperative for Educational Reform* (National Commission on Excellence in Education, 1983) and its economic rationale for radical changes in schools, assessments became an essential component of state and local improvement initiatives. Where testing programs previously were expected mainly to monitor student achievements, new and different demands were now placed on them. Assessments were expected to produce major changes in schools, provide a means for establishing that the changes occurred, and facilitate comparisons between and among states, the nation, and the world.

These assessments, however, were more often idiosyncratic than easily compared. Besides varying in context and subject, they served multiple purposes, produced results for multiple audiences, and were built on complex statistical and measurement methodologies. Questions surrounding proper interpretations of results and the technical properties of the assessments became as numerous as the surveys themselves. How was one to make sense of these results?

In this book, I hope to address important assessment themes, provide a perspective from which to view large-scale assessments, and lay the foundation for plausible interpretations of their results. Although I will express strong opinions about what I consider to be important issues embedded in this burgeoning arena, it is my desire to frame the questions fairly so the reader can judge the merit, or lack thereof, of the positions I take.

The Assessment Grid

It goes without saying that assessments focus on student academic achievements; that is, measures of student performance in varied school subjects form the basis of large-scale assessments. Purposes for the assessments and what is done with assessment results are, however, quite varied. Figure 1.1 is a grid that suggests major dimensions upon which assessments can be classified. I will use this grid to discuss various assessments, what they feature, how they are similar, and how they differ.

The grid contains 11 dimensions, each with different facets. Those dimensions and facets cover major ways that large-scale assessments can vary. The grid serves the following two main purposes: to describe differences between and among assessments and to raise issues that should be addressed about any assessment.

In its 1997 volume on accountability systems, the Educational Commission of the States (ECS) asserts that a complete system contains standards-based assessments, multiple indicators, rewards, and sanctions. Although my grid focuses on assessment with accountability as one facet, I will argue that a good assessment will have many more components than those envisaged by ECS in an accountability system. My focus is assessment; my hope is good assessment.

The grid progresses from top to bottom and assumes a logical (at least my logic) sequence. One should decide about the purposes and functions of an assessment before making decisions about whom to measure by what means. Decisions about what stakes to tie to the assessment, which particular outcomes to measure, and the particular kinds of assessments to use should be based on the purposes, functions, and targets of the assessment. Finally, decisions must be made about whether students are able to use technology during the assessment, what kinds of support they and their teachers get to increase the likelihood that they will be successful, and how all features of the assessment will be reported.

Each of the pieces of a coherent assessment will be logically tied to the remaining pieces. Reporting, for example, the last dimension should tie together each of the preceding dimensions and allow those who are interested to understand the purposes, targets, stakes, outcomes, and types of assessments used.

I will define and discuss each dimension, and I will focus on major issues and various attempts to solve the problems associated with an assessment. I

Assessment Grid

Purposes/	☐ Achievement	☐ Accountability	☐ Instruction
Functions:	☐ Monitor	☐ Certify	☐ Evaluate ☐ Compare
			☐ *Formative* *Summative*
Measures:	☐ Content	☐ Other	
	☐ *One* *More than one*		
Targets:	☐ Student	☐ Class/Teacher	☐ School ☐ District/State/Nation
	☐ Elementary	☐ Middle	☐ Secondary
Standards:	☐ Frameworks	☐ Content	☐ Proficiency ☐ OTL
	☐ Assessment		
Stakes:	☐ High	☐ Moderate	☐ Low
	☐ *Rewards* *Sanctions*		
Outcomes:	☐ Status	☐ Growth/Change	
		☐ *Cohort* *Longitudinal*	
Assessments:	☐ Traditional	☐ Performance	
	☐ *Multiple Choice* *Norm Referenced*	☐ *Constructed Response* *Performance Events* *Writing on Demand* *Portfolio*	
Technology	☐ Calculators	☐ Word Processors	☐ Adaptive Devices ☐ Other
Support:	☐ Students	☐ Teachers	☐ Staff
	☐ *Tutoring* *Summer School* *Other*	☐ *Staff Development*	
Reporting:	☐ Students/Parents	☐ Class/Teacher	☐ School ☐ Public

Figure 1.1. Assessment Grid

Kifer, E., *Large-Scale Assessments: Dimensions, Dilemmas, and Policy.* Copyright © 2001, Corwin Press, Inc.

hope the astute reader with a special interest in a particular assessment will be able to say something such as the following:

> Our assessment monitors reading achievement, focuses on elementary students, is based on three major content standards, has moder-

ate stakes attached to it, estimates a student's status on an assessment that is primarily performance based, provides additional support through tutoring, and reports to students, parents, and the public.

Someone else's favorite assessment might be a certification examination for accountability purposes with measures of reading, writing, and mathematics; focuses on high school students; uses proficiency standards; high stakes; includes longitudinal measures of change; and/or traditional assessments without any additional assistance or support for students. The reports may go only to students and parents.

Using the Grid

To show how the grid works and to set the stage for further discussions, I chose three examples. The first is the International Association for the Evaluation of Educational Achievement (IEA) and its most recent study, the Third International Mathematics and Science Study (TIMSS). The second is the National Assessment of Educational Progress (NAEP), and the third is the Kentucky Instructional Results Information System (KIRIS).

I have additional reasons for the choices. I suppose the first is that I feel reasonably familiar with the assessments. Each in its own way, however, has influenced the kinds of assessments that are practiced in the United States. They also set the stage for more detailed descriptions later in the book.

I chose IEA because of its early experience with large-scale international surveys and its desire to find things that worked. It has conducted numerous assessments containing both typical outcome measures and literally hundreds of background and process variables. The latter were used to try to explain differences among international systems. TIMSS, the latest and largest IEA survey, is included because it is recent and has been well publicized.

Because IEA's search is for variables that explain achievement differences, it focuses both on outcomes (ends) and inputs (means). The studies are based on what I think is a proper notion: Ends and means are inextricably entwined. One cannot change schools without dealing with both.

I choose NAEP because it, too, has influenced large-scale assessments both in the United States and abroad. It is interesting also because how it has changed since its inception in the 1960s is a kind of road map to new views of what assessments should be. From its initial, rather humble start, NAEP's attempts to assess what U.S. children and adults know and can do set standards for future assessments.

NAEP monitors student achievements. As I will argue later, I believe that is a proper, defensible function of an assessment.

I chose Kentucky because it was one of the first, if not the first, modern attempt at *Payment by Results* (Rapple, 1994) with a strong and high-stakes school accountability system as part of its assessment. That system has been in place almost 10 years. What it attempted to do and how it has changed is fodder for several of my subsequent discussions.

In some ways, Kentucky was the first state on the block to attempt complex assessments to change or reform schools. Being the first, it has been able to make mistakes and correct them. I wonder aloud whether those corrections are the right ones.

I begin each of the short stories about these three assessments with, at least, a passing glance to the past. I do not claim that this is history. It would be better if it were. Nevertheless, it is important to be reminded that sometimes we believe what we are doing is new and different when, in fact, it may be old and similar.

International Association for the Evaluation of Educational Achievement

Although other organizations conducted international assessments, the IEA was the major player in this arena. It conducted its first survey in the 1960s in mathematics (Husen, 1967). Since that time, it has assessed students, teachers, and other school personnel in studies focusing on topics such as reading (Thorndike, 1973), literature (Purves, 1973), science (Comber & Keeves, 1973), civics education (Torney, Oppenheim, & Farnen, 1975), classroom environments (Anderson, Ryan, & Shapiro, 1989), French as a foreign language (Carroll, 1975), and English as a foreign language (Lewis & Massad, 1975). It conducted a Second International Mathematics Study (SIMS) in the 1980s (see, e.g., Burstein, 1994; McKnight et al., 1987) and TIMSS in the 1990s (see Beaton, 1996; Martin et al., 1997; Schmidt, McKnight, Cogan, Jakwerth, & Houang, 1999; Schmidt, McKnight, & Raizen, 1997). In addition, in the 1990s it assessed computers and technology (Pelgrum & Plomp, 1993) and again, reading (Binkley & Rust, 1994).

IEA studies are collaborative efforts between countries and educational systems. Research institutes in participating educational systems work together to produce these complex surveys. Through these cooperative efforts, IEA deals effectively with such problems as translating from language to language, standardizing survey questions and research forms, establishing rules for valid participation, and defining research variables with common meanings.

Known for its adherence to high standards for sampling and data collection, IEA places a premium on standardizing methodology to permit comparisons between educational systems that are as valid as possible. IEA surveys emphasize outcomes of education and make inferences about their relations to variables describing school inputs and practices. Of particular interest in

IEA studies is finding predictive models that operate across contexts to produce desirable educational outcomes.

IEA and School Reform

IEA is a search for effective alternatives to common practice. Variations among international educational systems are the grist of the IEA mill and the hope for improving educational practices. As Foshay, Thorndike, Hotyat, Pidgeon, and Walker (1962) stated, "If custom and law define what is educationally allowable within a nation, the educational systems beyond one's national boundaries suggest what is educationally possible" (p. 15).

Because of its uniqueness on the international stage, IEA believes that it is a part of the broader conversation about school reform. Purves (1989) edited a book that succinctly reported findings believed to be important in fostering change and improvement in U.S. schools. Just as important, the book contained warnings about the limitations of jumping too rapidly to conclusions about results when they are not in a proper context. The findings and warnings remain, I believe, appropriate ways to think about education, reform, and assessment.

Westbury (1989), for example, noted one call for reform in the United States: more demanding curricula. Through analyses of IEA mathematics data, he suggested that the issue might not be more demanding curriculum, but rather giving more children opportunities to experience our best curriculum. The United States differentiates its mathematics (and other) curriculum more than most other systems in the international arena. For example, in eighth-grade mathematics, some students are exposed to mainly algebra content, and others may not be exposed to algebra at all. Westbury argued for looking more deeply than differences between average scores between countries and finding patterns (mainly in the curriculum) that help one to understand those differences.

IEA studies have identified other variables related to the curriculum that appear to influence achievement results. The amount of time devoted to a subject, the opportunity to learn (OTL) a subject, and lack of tracking of students (putting students in classes based on hypothesized differences in ability) are three such crucial variables (Kifer, 1989). Carroll (1975) presented a series of analyses that, over educational systems, related the number of years of studying French to average performance in reading, writing, and listening. Carroll estimated that it took the average student 6 to 7 years to attain a "satisfactory and high level" of performance. (This kind of standards-based interpretation of test scores will be discussed later.) That amount of time can be reduced if the student were fortunate enough to (a) have a fluent teacher (it reduces the amount of time needed by almost a year), (b) be taught mainly in French (an effect of a year and a half), and (c) have serious aspirations to learn French (an effect of about a half of a year of instruction). It is important to allocate a sufficient time for learning, but it is equally important to make good use of that time.

Comber and Keeves (1973) depicted a strong relationship between the IEA measure, OTL, and performance in science. Their findings have been replicated in other IEA surveys as well. OTL is a measure generated by teachers in IEA surveys that is an attempt to describe what material has been covered in that teacher's class. Each teacher is asked to rate the test questions (items) on the test in terms of whether the material needed to answer the question correctly was taught in their classroom. The measure is an attempt to determine whether the part of the curriculum that was intended to be implemented was actually implemented in classrooms. McKnight et al. (1987) with SIMS and, more recently, Schmidt et al. (1999) with TIMSS, have discussed the effects of OTL on achievement.

Tracking, putting students perceived to have different abilities or prior achievements in specific classes, and differentiating curriculum are linked in international studies to achievement (Kifer, 1989). The more and earlier one places students into tracks, the lower the achievement. The more differentiated the curriculum, the lower the achievement. Comparisons between the performance of Japanese students versus those in seven other systems suggest that more students participating in more mathematics is related to higher performance. Concretely, Japanese students, whose achievement was exemplary, were exposed to more mathematics on the international eighth-grade test. Furthermore, they have a common mathematics curriculum for all students. Hence, they exposed more mathematics to more students than did the other systems (Kifer, 1994).

Finally, according to Anderson and Postlethwaite (1989), IEA findings have implications for pedagogy. The authors maintain that IEA studies support Berliner's (1987) notions of classroom instruction, which included OTL, students' engagement in learning, students' experiences of success, pacing, structuring, and monitoring.

Third International Mathematics and Science Study

IEA's latest and largest foray is the TIMSS. Patrick Forgione (U.S. Department of Education, 1998a), in the commissioner's statement preceding the final volume of a series portraying TIMSS international results, says,

> The Third International Mathematics and Science Study (TIMSS) is the largest, most comprehensive, and most rigorous international study of schools and student achievement ever conducted. . . . The scope of TIMSS is unprecedented in the annals of education research. The international project involved the testing of more than one-half

million students in mathematics and science at three grade levels in 41 countries. (p. 5)

By now, most persons know the general pattern of results of TIMSS: U.S. 4th-grade students do well in mathematics, 8th-grade students are about average, and 12th-grade students' performance is low. In science, there is a similar pattern except that 4th-grade students in the United States rank near the top.

TIMSS was large—the largest IEA study ever. Imagine the logistic difficulties of administering assessments to more than half a million students, translating instruments into a multitude of languages, and keeping track of responses for a set of complicated statistical analyses. Furthermore, TIMSS did not limit itself to rather easily administered multiple-choice questions. It contained open-ended questions (constructed response) and hands-on assessments (performance assessments). Finally, TIMSS collected and is analyzing a series of videotapes of teachers delivering instruction in three international systems (Germany, Japan, and the United States). Excerpts of those tapes have been created for scrutiny by interested practitioners (National Center for Education Statistics, 1997).

TIMSS data will be analyzed for years to come, I hope. However, to date much of its reporting has been achievement comparisons between international systems; that is, the focus has been on outcomes or ends, not the means. It has not yet tackled the traditional variety of issues about schools and schooling found in earlier IEA surveys. As one TIMSS document states, "It is too early in the process of data analysis to provide strong evidence to suggest factors that may be related to the patterns of performance described here" (U.S. Department of Education, 1998b, p. 54). Rather, there are a series of comparisons between average levels of achievement that produce the findings cited above. Much speculation is attached to those differences but there is little or no reported empirical work that relates different practices to levels of achievement. Predictive models—SIMS used a longitudinal design and elaborate teacher questionnaires to link what teachers do to performance—have not yet been generated for TIMSS.

The U.S. national reports of TIMSS are more traditionally IEA. *A Splintered Vision* (Schmidt et al., 1997) thoroughly investigates curriculum issues and comes up with the pithy phrase that the U.S. mathematics curriculum is "a mile wide and an inch deep." McKnight et al.'s (1987) aphorism for the SIMS version was a curriculum that was a series of one-night stands.

The notions that U.S. curriculum has far too many topics and none that are dealt with in depth is a recurring finding of international studies. As I will indicate later, I believe similar problems are evident in the various kinds of standards we use in our assessments. Breadth, not depth, is a general problem.

Just recently, Schmidt et al. (1999) of the TIMSS U.S. National Center reported more detailed results from TIMSS. They also found that curriculum matters and access or participating in the curriculum matters as well. They also include a set of conjectures about the relationships among achievement outcomes and textbooks, the amount of time devoted to subject matter, the context of pedagogy, and particularities of U.S. schools (i.e., high mobility rates).

The Grid for IEA-TIMSS

Because IEA has conducted many studies, the grids would not be similar in all cases. There would be, however, similarities between them. Hence, the TIMSS grid, Figure 1.2.

TIMSS assessed achievement to compare international educational systems in more than one content area. The targets were students and national systems. The assessment included a curriculum framework, was low stakes, and measured the status of achievement. It had varied ways to assess, including both traditional and performance assessments, and it allowed the use of calculators and provided no support or training for students to perform well. Its main reporting was to publics of the various participating countries.

National Assessment of Educational Progress

What Is NAEP?

NAEP, the nation's report card, is the only U.S. assessment that produces representative national results of achievement outcomes. The assessments produce both current results and trends in achievement over time, some of which extend to the late 1960s. Therefore, it is potentially useful to a variety of educational audiences and institutions.

The recent and unprecedented exposure for NAEP and the demand for its results makes it easy to forget that a national assessment in the United States is rather new. NAEP, it is said, started about 30 years ago when Ralph Tyler took a memorandum to John Tukey and Fred Mosteller. The document contained Tyler's thoughts on how one might assess educational outcomes—what students and adults know and can do—across the United States. Tukey and Mosteller were to comment on it and give technical advice, which they did then and for years after as members of the NAEP technical panel (for a history of early NAEP, see Hazlett, 1973).

The Tyler memo defined the substance and techniques of NAEP for more than a decade. From 1970 through 1982, the Educational Commission of the States (ECS) conducted two or three NAEP surveys a year. Since 1983, the Educational Testing Service (ETS) has conducted NAEP surveys (see Messick, Beaton, & Lord, 1983, for a rationale that changed NAEP). Figure 1.3 shows NAEP assessments from their inception in 1969 until 1996.

Assessment Grid

Purposes/ Functions:	[X] Achievement	[ ] Accountability	[ ] Instruction	
	[ ] Monitor	[ ] Certify	[ ] Evaluate *Formative* *Summative*	[X] Compare

Measures:	[X] Content	[ ] Other
	[X] *One*	
	[X] *More than one*	

Targets:	[X] Student	[ ] Class/Teacher	[ ] School	[X] District/State/Nation
	[X] Elementary	[X] Middle	[X] Secondary	

Standards:	[X] Frameworks	[ ] Content	[ ] Proficiency	[ ] OTL
	[ ] Assessment			

Stakes:	[ ] High	[ ] Moderate	[X] Low
	[ ] *Rewards* *Sanctions*		

Outcomes:	[X] Status	[ ] Growth/Change
		[ ] *Cohort* *Longitudinal*

Assessments:	[X] Traditional	[X] Performance
	[X] *Multiple Choice* [ ] *Norm Referenced*	[X] *Constructed Response* [X] *Performance Events* [ ] *Writing on Demand* [ ] *Portfolio*

Technology	[ ] Calculators	[ ] Word Processors	[ ] Adaptive Devices	[ ] Other

Support:	[ ] Students	[ ] Teachers	[ ] Staff
	[ ] *Tutoring* *Summer School* *Other*	[ ] *Staff Development*	

Reporting:	[ ] Students/Parents	[ ] Class/Teacher	[ ] School	[X] Public

Figure 1.2. The International Association for the Evaluation of Educational Achievement (IEA) Third International Mathematics and Science Study (TIMSS) Assessment Grid

Tyler would be, I imagine, surprised by the success of his conception. In the last 25 years or so, NAEP has conducted more than 60 separate surveys (or about triple that if each age and grade survey were to count individually) in a score of content areas.

NAEP Assessments -- 1969 - 1996

Year	Reading	Writing	Mathematics	Science	Others		
1969-70	X			X	Literature		
1970-71					Social Studies	Music	
1971-72							
1972-73			X	X			
1973-74		X			Career Dev.		
1974-75	X				Art	Basic Skills	
1975-76			X*		Social Studies	Citizenship	
1976-77	X*			X*	Life Skills	Health*	
1977-78			X		Consumer Econ		
1978-79		X			Art	Music	
1979-80	X				Art*		
1980-81							
1981-82	X			X*	Social Studies		
Move from ECS to ETS: 1) from age to age/grade samples; 2) from exercises to scales to standards; 3) stopped assessing 17 year olds out of school and adults; and, 4) stopped yearly assessments.							
1984	X**	X**					
1985					Adult Literacy		
1986	X**		X**	X**	Computer	US History*	Literacy*
1987							
1988	X**	X**	X**	X***	Civics**	US History	Doc Literacy*
1989							
Move to a trial state assessment							
1990	X**	X***	X**	X**	State Math		
1991							
1992	X**	X**	X**	X***	State Math	State Reading	
1993							
1994	X**	X***	X***	X***	Geography	US History	State Reading
1995							
Move to trial district assessments							
1996	X***	X***	X**	X**	State Science	State Math	District

*Less than a full assessment ** Full assessment plus long term trend assessment ***Long term trend assessment

Figure 1.3. NAEP Assessments from 1969 to 1996

During its first phase, the Educational Commission of the States assessments included both the core subjects of reading, writing, mathematics, and science, and other curricular areas such as art, health, and citizenship. Surveys, especially of the core areas, were repeated on a regular basis (usually every 5 years) so one could determine if there were changes across time on the outcomes.

The assessments measured a variety of outcomes and included varied samples of persons. Pupils aged 9, 13, and 17 years in school and 17-year-olds and adults out of school were the NAEP populations. Comparisons of results across age groups and between those in school and those not in school provided a means to look critically at important outcomes of schooling.

Each person in early NAEP surveys responded to a subset of exercises. With such sampling of exercises, one could cover more content (ask more questions), but not tax those who participated in the surveys (initially students spent no more than 1 hour answering questions; i.e., responding to exercises). These exercises were the foundation of early NAEP surveys. Although providing comprehensive coverage of content, they were also the unit of analysis and reporting. Exercises focused on skill and knowledge domains considered to be important. The results on the exercises were the means to describe the nation's performance.

Changes in NAEP

In 1983, NAEP moved from ECS to the Educational Testing Service (ETS). The move changed the nature of NAEP assessments in fundamental ways (Beaton & Zwick, 1992). Probably the major change was moving from the finite unit of an exercise (or question) to the scaling of items or tasks. Rather than report percentages of persons who could do a task or averages of those percentages over tasks, the new NAEP created a scale on which to report the results (Beaton & Johnson, 1992). Scores from year to year and on different surveys were assigned values on a scale from 100 to 500 (there are surveys that have a scale from 100 to 300). Except for presentation purposes, item results were no longer published; instead, average scores, either overall or by subgroup, were computed on this new scale.

Other changes to NAEP during the last decade include dropping the assessment of out of school populations, substituting assessments every 4 years for yearly ones (although assessments in particular content areas are more frequent), including grade and age samples, and assessing states and school districts. The latter assessments of states and school districts are recent and represent new and uncharted territories. They were conducted, however, amidst a substantial amount of controversy (see Alexander & James, 1987; Ferrara & Thornton, 1988; Glaser & Linn, 1992; Haertel, 1989, 1991; Koretz, 1989, 1991; Phillips, 1991; Wolf, 1992).

The chronology shows a heavy emphasis on core curricular areas and assessments of trends in those areas. In recent years, there have been even more frequent trend assessments in the core areas, but fewer forays into other content areas. The newest arena for NAEP is assessing states or districts (Alexander & James, 1987). This began with trial state assessments in 1990, continued with district assessments in 1996, and is likely to remain even as NAEP is redesigned (Johnson, Lazer, & O'Sullivan, 1997).

The National Assessment
Governing Board (NAGB)

The purposes of NAEP are clear: to assess what students know and can do. The NAGB was formed in the 1990s to conduct the national assessment and report on its results. The board has instituted a set of procedures that define the characteristics of each survey. The first define an assessment framework that more or less serves the purposes of articulating the content and processes that survey questions should address. The framework is not quite a curriculum guide and not quite a test specification document. It guides the assessments but it is not related to a particular curriculum (Mullis, 1992; NAGB, 1993a, 1993b, 1995a, 1995b). Rather, it is a consensus document detailing what students should know and should be able to do. Notice the very important change in language: NAGP wants NAEP to measure what students should know and should be able to do rather than the original intention of what students and adults know and are able to do.

NAGB also instituted the use of achievement levels to serve as standards of student performance. These achievement levels, what I call *proficiency standards* and will discuss later, define basic, advanced, and proficient levels of performance on the NAEP assessments. That innovation, too, was controversial (see Bourque & Hambleton, 1993; Burstein et al., 1993; National Academy of Education, 1993; Stufflebeam, Jaeger, & Scriven, 1991).

From the beginning, NAEP has included a variety of item types in its surveys (Tyler, 1970). Large-scale performance assessment probably began with the original NAEP and continues today in the form of what are called *constructed response* and *extended constructed response* items (see, e.g., Dossey, Mullis, & Jones, 1993).

Technical Prowess of NAEP

Throughout its history, NAEP has been technically innovative and rigorous. It is the only nationally representative assessment because its early emphasis on impeccable sampling (Hazlett, 1973) continues today (Johnson & Rust, 1992). It introduced matrix sampling, Item Response Theory, and Balanced Incomplete Block (BIB) spiraling to large-scale assessments. See Figures 1.4 and the two boxed inserts for an explanation of matrix sampling and Item Response Theory. Both techniques were first used, I believe, by NAEP in large-scale surveys.

Because of the special nature of its sampling, Mislevy (1993; Mislevy, Beaton, Kaplan, & Sheehan, 1992a, 1992b) showed how multiple imputation (a statistical technique first used to account for missing data in responses) aids NAEP analyses. NAEP lead large-scale testing away from predominately multiple-choice items by introducing open-ended exercises in the original NAEP and constructed and extended constructed response items in the present NAEP (Mullis, 1992). It also invented statistical scaling methods to deal with the new response formats (Muraki, 1992, 1993).

	Traditional Assessment (each student takes all questions)	*Matrix or Item Sampling (five forms)*
Test size	30 questions	30 questions
Sample size	300 students per question	60 students per question
Information about how many items	30	150
Imprecision	× amount of error	About 2 × amount of error
Student scores	Estimated on 30 questions	Estimated on 30 different questions
School averages	Estimated on 30 questions	Estimated on 150 questions
School average sample size	300	60
Subarea averages (sex)	Estimated on 30/5 = 6 questions	Estimated on 150/5 = 30 questions
Advantages	Slightly more precision	More content coverage
Disadvantage	Know more about less	Less precision

Figure 1.4. Matrix or Item Sampling

Matrix Sampling

Item or matrix sampling is a way to get more information about student performance in a subject matter (e.g., mathematics) in a fixed amount of time. Suppose you have 1 hour to assess students. You want the assessment to measure six subareas of a particular content. You are not so concerned about individual scores, but wish to have good information about how well schools are doing. The school has 300 students. Finally, suppose that you know that students can do about 30 questions in an hour. Figure 1.4 describes the features or item sampling and the benefits derived from it.

In this scenario, an assessment could gather information about students' performance on five times as could many questions in the same 1-hour testing session. Although the traditional testing would allow one to compare student's scores because each of the 300 students answered the same 30 questions, it would be limited to those questions. Item sampling would sacrifice the comparability of student scores to get a larger sample of the content domain (e.g., mathematics). One hour of testing would give information on 150 different questions. For comparisons between schools, then, there would be 150 questions worth of information. The advantages of the item sampling are even more evident if one wants sub-test scores (e.g., arithmetic, measurement, geometry, statistics, and algebra). In the traditional case, there would be five questions per subtest. With item sampling there would be 30 items per subtest equal to the total number of mathematics questions under traditional assessment procedures.

Item Response Theory

Most, if not all, large-scale assessments now use, in some fashion, models based on Item Response Theory (IRT). Those models, often called *strong true score* models, have statistical advantages over what they replaced, Classical Test Theory. The primary advantage of IRT models, in a nutshell, is if the models are appropriate, any set of test questions (items) can be used to estimate how well a student would do if he or she answered all of the items.

The notion of a model being appropriate has a precise, statistical meaning: The items measure one, and only one, dimension of the person. That dimension is called a *latent trait*. When a model fits, there is only one latent attribute that is being measured. When each and every item in an item pool measures the same latent trait, it is a matter of indifference to students what items they respond to. They can be scored as though they had taken all of the items.

Metaphors can be misleading, but let me try one. Suppose you wanted to measure someone's height. You have no tape measure but you have a pile of sticks of different overall length, each of which has equally spaced notches on it. You could measure a person's height by taking any of the sticks, placing them against the person, and counting how many notches were equal to the distance between the bottom of that person's feet and the top of his or her head. It would not matter which stick you used because each of the sticks had notches the same distance apart. In IRT language, calibrating an item set is comparable to cutting notches in the sticks. Once the items have been notched, you can use any set of them to measure the same latent dimension.

IRT models, combined with item sampling, can be powerful ways to get information about students' performances in a cost-effective way (more information for the time and money). The models also are useful in tracking performance over time and calibrating new questions (equating) as they enter an assessment.

Perceived Problems of NAEP

Although its technical strengths are both considerable and recognized, throughout its history NAEP has been plagued by not having resolved one major substantive problem: to make the results more understandable and accessible to those interested in educational matters. Recent criticisms include Zorn's (1994) criticism of the reading assessment, Silver and Kenney's (1993) criticism of the relationship of the 1992 mathematics assessment to the National Council of the Teachers of Mathematics (NCTM) standards, and general questions about how NAEP scores should be interpreted (Forsyth, 1991).

NAEP Scores

Most educational testing takes the form of giving individuals a collection of questions, marking the questions, and summing the correct answers to get a score. That score may be placed in a variety of contexts (e.g., the score is at the 67th percentile based on a national norm group) so the test taker has a way to determine how the score ranks.

NAEP has never produced scores of this type. When ECS conducted the assessment, student scores were inappropriate because each student responded to relatively few exercises. Score reporting was based on the proportions of students who answered a question or completed an exercise correctly (Tyler, 1970). Such proportions were reported for a variety of background characteristics, including gender, ethnicity, and region of the country.

With the change to ETS, scores are reported as on an IRT scale (a statistical notion I discuss earlier). Sophisticated statistical methods (Mislevy et al., 1992a, 1992b) are used to compute means, subgroup means, and proportions at or above certain achievement levels. These derived scores, called *proficiencies*, are placed on a scale from 0 to 500.

Each of these scoring schemes has received criticism. With the ECS scheme, it was difficult to report succinctly when there were so many questions and exercises. Item response methods, now used by NAEP, produce scores that are highly abstract and difficult to attach a meaning to.

Constructing NAEP Assessments: Then and Now

I think it is interesting to compare the two approaches to test construction. Tyler (Hazlett, 1973) noted that total scores are abstract entities that are difficult to interpret. He believed that proper score interpretations were tied to the educational objective that a question or exercise purported to measure. ECS

NAEP, therefore, generated items and exercises that met several criteria. Each item should be the following:

1. Defensible in the eyes of content experts
2. Something taught by schools
3. Understood by informed lay persons

In addition, the assessment should include items and exercises grouped by thirds for any age level. The *thirds* were grouped items that could be answered correctly by the following groups:

1. Most persons of that age
2. Few persons of that age
3. A typical person of that age

In this scheme, how difficult an item was (the proportion of persons who can answer it correctly) was separated conceptually from its educational importance, and by varying the difficulty of the questions, one had built-in comparisons of what an age group knew and could do.

In the new NAEP, one starts with a framework (NAGB, 1993a, 1993b, 1995a, 1995b) that is arrived at through a consensus process using persons of varied backgrounds and educational interests. Typically, the frameworks contain the following two dimensions: a content dimension and a behavioral or cognitive dimension. For example, in the 1994 geography assessment, the content dimension includes space and place, environment and society, and spatial dynamics and connections (NAGB, 1993b). The cognitive dimension includes knowing, understanding, and applying. Items or questions are generated that fit into each of the dimensions with NAGB making a determination of how much testing time is allotted to each dimension.

Changes Over Time: NAEP Trends

Arguably, NAEP's most important function is monitoring achievement patterns over time. Such trends, some extending almost 30 years, provide valuable contexts from which to understand achievement outcomes of our schools. Berliner and Biddle (1995) used stable NAEP trends in mathematics to counter claims made in the 1980s that there had been huge declines in academic performance. Average Scholastic Achievement Test (SAT) scores dropped during that decade because, many critics suggested, there was a general decline in the quality of schooling. Berliner and Biddle pointed out that because SAT scores do not come from nationally representative samples but NAEP scores do, the latter are much better indicators.

Of course, NAEP trend data are potentially problematic, too. Zwick (1992) deals with statistical, psychometric, and other issues related by trends over such a long period. For example, curriculum changes threaten the validity of NAEP trends. If a curriculum has changed over the years with some topics or skills being added and other being discarded and the NAEP test has not changed, then the trend data may be erroneously tracking performance.

To respond to these potential threats to the validity of trend results, NAGB has instituted a policy of having two kinds of trends. The first keeps previous assessments in the long-term trends exactly as they are and reports those results. The second set of trends begins when a new framework is developed in a particular content area and continues until there is a new framework.

State and District NAEP

Alexander and James (1987) recommended strongly that NAEP begin state-by-state and district-level assessments.

> Today state and local school administrators are encountering a rising public demand for thorough information of the quality of their schools, allowing comparison with data from other states and districts and with their own historical records. Responding to calls for greater accountability and for substantive school improvements, state officials have increasingly turned to the national assessment for assistance. (Alexander & James, 1987, p. 11)

Such assessments and comparisons were considered early in NAEP, but were strongly objected to by a number of professional groups. Among other things, critics voiced concerns about a national test and possibilities of it turning into demands for a national curriculum (Hazlett, 1973).

State-by-state assessments began in 1990 but not without controversy. Phillips (1991) provided a rationale for state participation in NAEP in terms of how valid and reliable comparisons could help states understand how well they were doing. Koretz (1989, 1991) criticized state NAEP on a variety of grounds including that the costs outweighed the benefits. Ferrara and Thornton (1988) echoed the early concern of state NAEP beginning a trend toward national curricula. Wolf (1992) wondered about its usefulness, and Glaser and Linn (1992) gave the initial state-by-state comparisons a mixed review. Haertel (1991) was equivocal as well, wondering how this new foray would interfere with NAEP's original intent and purposes.

State NAEP is, I think, a fixture of our assessment scene. It is here to stay because it is being used by states to make arguments for further changes in schooling or for the success of existing innovations. NAEP results become a major player in state-by-state comparisons because they are based on representative samples of students. They are problematic because the assessments upon which they are based do not necessarily reflect the curricula students' experience. I will deal with those issues later in this book.

Reporting NAEP Results

How best to report NAEP results is an enduring question. As I stated earlier, the young NAEP had difficulty because it reported results exercise by exercise. With so many different exercises, it was difficult to produce succinct reports. The new NAEP has difficulty as well. The NAEP scale is based on terribly complex calculations. The achievement or proficiency levels have been soundly criticized. State-by-state comparisons have not entered the public conversation without controversy either.

Having said all of that, there is an amazing amount of information about NAEP that is available to the public. There is information available from the beginning to end of each recent NAEP assessment. NAGB publishes the frameworks. The results of a survey are published in short and long forms. Particular aspects of findings of a survey are published as separate, small pieces. NAEP CD-ROMs are available that contain detailed results and exercises such as performances of students in the recent arts assessment. Technical manuals are available describing each of the surveys. There is a robust program of what is called *secondary analysis* (analyzing data in more depth to get results about a limited set of issues) of NAEP data. Finally, there are Web sites for both NCES and NAGB with incredible amounts of information for the interested public. It is possible to get to know NAEP well through its publication agenda.

Of particular interest in reporting NAEP results is the release of the 1997 arts report card on CD-ROM. For the first time, I believe, the National Center for Education Statistics has been able to provide a multimedia presentation of results. Those who are interested can see videotaped clips of what students were asked to be able to do. It is possible to see the dancing, hear the music, and scrutinize results from that innovative assessment.

NAEP on the Assessment Grid

The assessment grid for NAEP, Figure 1.5, is a bit more complicated than that of TIMSS. Because NAEP conducts so many surveys, I decided to give a kind of composite summary with additional explanations where they were called for.

Whether it is the old NAEP that aimed to assess what students and adults knew and could do or the new NAEP that aims to assess what students should know and be able to do, the purpose and function of NAEP is to monitor

Assessment Grid

Purposes/	[X] Achievement	[ ] Accountability	[ ] Instruction	
Functions:	[X] Monitor	[ ] Certify	[ ] Evaluate *Formative* [ ] *Summative*	[ ] Compare
Measures:	[X] Content [ ] *One* *More than one*	[ ] Other		
Targets:	[X] Student [X] Elementary	[ ] Class/Teacher [X] Middle	[ ] School [X] Secondary	[X] District/State/Nation
Standards:	[X] Frameworks [ ] Assessment	[ ] Content	[X] Proficiency	[ ] OTL
Stakes:	[ ] High [ ] *Rewards* *Sanctions*	[ ] Moderate	[X] Low	
Outcomes:	[X] Status	[X] Growth/Change [X] *Cohort* [ ] *Longitudinal*		
Assessments:	[X] Traditional [ ] *Multiple Choice* [ ] *Norm Referenced*	[X] Performance [X] *Constructed Response* [X] *Performance Events* [X] *Writing on Demand* [ ] *Portfolio*		
Technology	[X] Calculators	[ ] Word Processors	[X] Adaptive Devices	[X] Other
Support:	[ ] Students [ ] *Tutoring* *Summer School* *Other*	[ ] Teachers [ ] *Staff Development*	[ ] Staff	
Reporting:	[ ] Students/Parents	[ ] Class/Teacher	[ ] School	[X] Public

Figure 1.5. A National Assessment of Educational Progress (NAEP) Assessment Grid

achievement. It does this by assessing one subject matter content at a time, with targets at each level of schooling (e.g., 4th, 8th, and 12th grades), depending on the survey, and sometimes states and districts. Its surveys are always based on frameworks, the results are reported in terms of proficiency standards, and the stakes are always low for the target students. Its assessments are mixed with some traditional measures and, depending on the survey, varied performance measures. It allows calculators on forms of the survey and attempts to accommodate students with varied devices. It has no way of providing help for students or teachers to do well on the survey. It is, therefore, limited in its power to influence what schools do. It can, however, through its national and international visibility and its influence on other assessments, indirectly effect change. It reports to the public, but it has many publics, such as educators, researchers, and policy makers, to name the most obvious.

The Kentucky Instructional Results and Information System

KIRIS Background

Kentucky's educational reform has an interesting and colorful context and recent history (for a detailed look at the Kentucky assessment, see Guskey, 1994). To see the Kentucky systems within the context of other kinds of assessments, such as the Oregon Teacher Work Sample; Dallas, Texas Value-Added Accountability System; and the Tennessee Value-Added Assessment System, see Millman (1997).

Kentucky was among the first states to institute a large-scale assessment as a way to reform schools. It did so because a 1990 legal opinion declared the commonwealth's system of public education to be unconstitutional (*Rose v Council for Better Education, Inc.*, 1989). The reform act had multiple features including more equal financing of schools, school councils for governing, and ungraded primary schools. What turned out to be its most visible component, however, was a new statewide assessment of student performance and school outcomes. Not only would there be a new statewide assessment but also it would contain high stakes to reward or sanction schools based on their performance. In addition, there was an emphasis on continuous assessments that were hypothesized to influence instructional practices.

The law placed a special emphasis on performance assessments, as opposed to multiple-choice tests, which were to play a central role in the reform of Kentucky schools. The performance measures were to reflect learning goals defined and elaborated by a Council on School Performance Standards (1989). Later in the book, documents such as these will be referred to as containing content standards or content frameworks, which defined what students should learn.

When fully developed, the assessment was to be primarily performance based. Performance demonstrations of desired outcomes were to be the most heavily weighted component of a statewide, school-level, accountability system. The assessment was to be powerful enough to change instructional patterns; that is, it was envisaged that daily instructional work would contain experiences similar to those that were tested. Instruction and assessment were to be seamless.

Procedures for Implementing Performance Assessment

There were several specifications regarding the implementation of the assessment. Content standards were developed by a consensual approach of educators, teachers, and lay persons. Information about the standards and new curricula were to be disseminated to local districts and schools. The assessment that began in 1992 was to grow larger over time until it was completely in place during the 1995-1996 school year.

Initially, reading, mathematics, writing, science, and social science were to be assessed in Grades 4, 8, and 12. The testing was designed to provide national comparisons as well as accountability information. The law implied that the national comparisons would be accomplished by designing the assessment to mimic NAEP. In fact, the law stated that the assessment should be similar to the NAEP, although it did not spell out what *similar* meant. Initially, the tests contained a variety of measures, including some multiple-choice items, performance events, and portfolio tasks. Later, the assessment was to be mainly a performance assessment. Results of the assessment combined with other school variables such as expectations for success, attendance rates, and drop-out rates were combined to form a school-level accountability system.

Features of the Statewide Assessment

The Assessment Design

Figure 1.6 captures the essence of the initial assessment scheme. As shown in the figure, the assessment is embedded in the commonwealth's six broad learning goals. It contains two major strands: the accountability assessment and the continuous assessment.

Accountability Strand

Each school in the commonwealth was required to be a part of the accountability system. The following were three components in this assessment strand: (a) performance measurements, (b) portfolio tasks, and (c) transitional items and tasks. Assessments were to be conducted annually with an accountability decision made every 2 years.

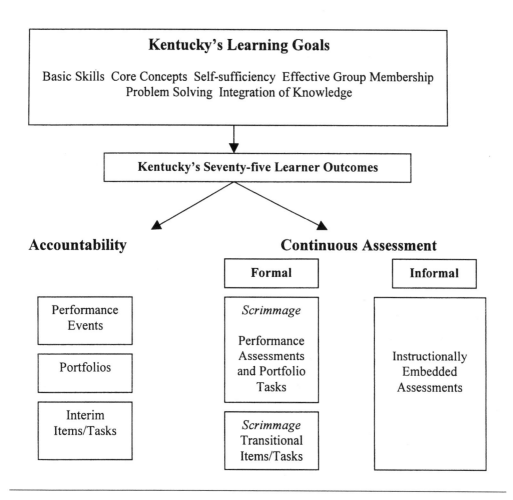

Assessment System – Original Plan
Kentucky Assessment

Kentucky's Learning Goals

Basic Skills Core Concepts Self-sufficiency Effective Group Membership
Problem Solving Integration of Knowledge

Kentucky's Seventy-five Learner Outcomes

Accountability   **Continuous Assessment**

                                   Formal   **Informal**

Performance   *Scrimmage*
Events
                                   Performance
                                   Assessments   Instructionally
Portfolios   and Portfolio   Embedded
                                   Tasks   Assessments

Interim   *Scrimmage*
Items/Tasks   Transitional
                                   Items/Tasks

Figure 1.6. Kentucky Assessment

Continuous Assessment Strand

The continuous assessment strand had two components, both of which were
voluntary. The formal component was designed to give students in grades
other than Grades 4, 8, and 12 an opportunity to practice the types of activities
required in the accountability strand. The second component of the continuous assessment was related to day-by-day activities within classrooms. Here,
the kinds of products, performances, and activities that were part of a school's
instructional program were meant to be indistinguishable from the formal

assessment activities conducted annually in the accountability assessments. Students and teachers at all grade levels would be working together on things quite similar to what would be required in the assessment program. It was envisioned that teachers would be given exemplary materials to make instruction and assessment appear to be inseparable, that is, seamless. The emphasis on performance tasks was an attempt to make a test worth teaching.

Holding Schools Accountable

Schools, not students, were to be held accountable in the Kentucky assessment. Improvement had to be made every 2 years. Improvement was expected in not only cognitive areas measured by the performance assessments and more traditional tests but also in areas such as attendance, drop-out rates, transitions from school, and expectations for achievement.

The Model of School Accountability

During the spring of 1992, schools throughout the commonwealth were measured through a variety of means to establish a baseline from which to judge improvement. Two years later, they were to be held accountable for an increase in the percentage of successful students. Schools could be rewarded or sanctioned on the basis of their performance during the 2-year period.

The accountability formula weighs the assessment of six learning goals to arrive at a composite percentage of successful students in a school. That composite was, by law, to give more weight to the cognitive goals than to any of the other components.

Trimble (1994) discussed how Kentucky defined successful students in terms of proficiency levels (i.e., novice, apprentice, proficient, and distinguished), weighted student scores to get a school average, and then averaged those scores with the so-called noncognitive factors to come up with an accountability score for each school. What in the law was called a successful student was transformed into the various proficiency levels with a target of each student in a school being proficient in a 20-year span.

The bottom of Figure 1.7 shows the relationship between a baseline formed in the spring of 1992 and targets for achievement 2 years later. Each school was expected to improve given its initial status; that is, from its Time 1 baseline to its target.

How much a school was to improve (i.e., the calculation of the threshold value) was based on the estimated amount of growth that had to occur over 20 years. The rule was to subtract the Time 1 baseline from 100 and divide that difference by 10 (10 accountability periods of 2 years, each making the 20-year interval). For example, a school with a score of 50 would need to gain 5 points (100 − 50 divided by 10) per accountability period to reach the target. A school with an initial score of 30 would have to gain about 7 points

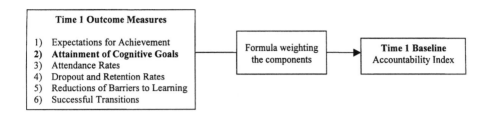

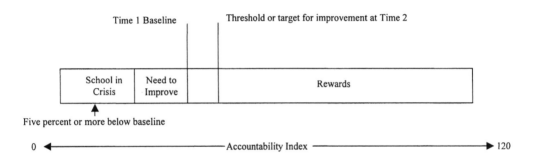

Figure 1.7. The Accountability Model for the Kentucky Assessment

(100 − 30 divided by 10) in that same period. The threshold was to be defined so that it was fair to each school, regardless of its initial status.

In 1994, at the end of the 2-year cycle, an accountability decision was to be made and a new target value, based on the accountability index, was to be estimated for each school. Schools that exceeded their threshold or target values by 1% or more were eligible for financial rewards. Schools that had an accountability index at or below their baseline were to be sanctioned. A decrease of up to 5% placed the school in a category where improvement was needed. Those schools developed a school improvement plan, were eligible to receive additional funding, and were assisted by a group of distinguished educators. A decrease of more than 5% placed a school in a crisis category. Sanctions for a school in crisis could include placing the State Department of Education in control of the school.

Primarily Performance Based

Because a full assessment system, primarily performance based, had to be in place by 1996, the assessment broadened in well-defined steps. The first was in terms of the components of the accountability strand. More performance events and portfolio tasks were planned in each subsequent year. Also, the proportion of those types of activities were to increase each year. Another kind of expansion was increasing the number of content areas measured and measuring all of the relevant goals.

The first segment of the assessment program was conducted in the spring of 1992. It has now been almost a decade since it began. Major changes have occurred that will be discussed later. Figure 1.8 shows how it looked, according to the assessment grid, when it started.

Kentucky on the Assessment Grid

KIRIS purposes were to improve achievement, hold schools accountable, and change instruction in the schools. It documented summative evaluations of achievement and other measures through an accountability system. Although it measured students, its real targets were elementary, middle, and senior high schools in the Commonwealth of Kentucky. It was based on content standards and reported scores based on proficiency standards. Despite its desire to change instruction, it had no OTL standards. The stakes were very high with rewards and sanctions based on an accountability formula. It measured differences or growth between student cohorts (e.g., one fourth-grade class this year and another fourth-grade class 2 years from now) with both traditional and performance assessments. It particularly emphasized portfolios. It allowed students to use calculators and word processors in certain conditions, and it attempted to include most students in the assessment by making accommodations. The system provided support for students in varied forms, but did little to help teachers change instruction. It reported to students, parents, schools, and the public.

Kentucky Redux

Kentucky's assessment system was large, complex, and ambitious. It aimed to do the following two, what now appear to be incompatible, things: provide a statewide, school-level, accountability system and produce dramatic changes in curriculum and instruction in public schools. In terms of the latter, it was based on the premise that exemplary assessment procedures would produce optimal instruction. Teaching to the assessments, it was believed, would not only produce increasingly higher test scores but also drive desirable instructional practices. There were twin goals of creating a test worth teaching to and teaching teachers how to do it.

Assessment Grid			
Purposes/ Functions:	☒ Achievement	☒ Accountability	☒ Instruction
	☐ Monitor	☐ Certify	☒ Evaluate / *Formative* / ☒ *Summative*	☐ Compare
Measures:	☒ Content	☒ Other	
	☐ *One* / ☒ *More than one*		
Targets:	☐ Student	☐ Class/Teacher	☒ School	☐ District/State/Nation
	☒ Elementary	☒ Middle	☒ Secondary	
Standards:	☐ Frameworks	☒ Content	☒ Proficiency	☐ OTL
	☐ Assessment			
Stakes:	☒ High	☐ Moderate	☐ Low	
	☒ *Rewards* / ☒ *Sanctions*			
Outcomes:	☐ Status	☒ Growth/Change		
		☒ *Cohort* / ☐ *Longitudinal*		
Assessments:	☒ Traditional	☒ Performance		
	☒ *Multiple Choice* / ☐ *Norm Referenced*	☒ *Constructed Response* / ☒ *Performance Events* / ☒ *Writing on Demand* / ☒ *Portfolio*		
Technology	☒ Calculators	☒ Word Processors	☒ Adaptive Devices	☒ Other
Support:	☒ Students	☐ Teachers	☐ Staff	
	☒ *Tutoring* / ☒ *Summer School* / ☒ *Other*	☐ *Staff Development*		
Reporting:	☒ Students/Parents	☒ Class/Teacher	☒ School	☒ Public

Figure 1.8. The Kentucky Instructional Results Information System (KIRIS) Assessment Grid

Kentucky's assessment has been thoroughly changed. If I were to complete an assessment grid for the new version, it would look much more traditional than the original assessment. Gone are much of the innovative assessments, and in their place are multiple-choice tests. Performance events are gone. The mathematics portfolio has been eliminated. A new accountability system has been designed and will be used in the near future.

Accountability as a Lightning Rod

As Yogi Berra might say, it started to change in the beginning. The Kentucky Department of Education literature emphasized the accountability system and ignored the continuous assessment. The continuous assessment became practice tests and the tests were used for accountability purposes. The original intent to help teachers integrate assessment activities with instructional ones was ignored.

A decision was also made to eliminate two of the outcomes or learning goals. The two that were eliminated were self-sufficiency and effective group membership. What remained were basic skills, core concepts, and problem solving. The latter, I assume, remained because they were more easily measured.

There were those of us who thought that foreign languages would be assessed as a part of the art and humanities portion of the assessment. Assessments in those areas were never conducted.

The first parts of the actual assessment to go were the performance events. Completely ignoring the fact that performance assessments were included in KIRIS to change instruction (the continuous assessment), it was decided they were not sufficiently reliable and valid to be part of the accountability model. This occurred despite the fact that the performance events were well received by teachers and considered extraordinarily successful in the classroom. Observers noted how enthusiastically students approached the tasks, despite the fact that they were very challenging.

Another innovative part of the assessment, the mathematics portfolio, went by the wayside, too. Again, the argument was that it was not technically (reliable and valid) strong enough be a part of the accountability.

As I write this, Kentucky continues to tinker with the accountability system and continues to ignore the importance of assisting teachers. Multiple-choice items are getting a larger proportion of testing time. The original intent of the assessment is barely recognizable.

Two Different Things

Kentucky's assessment is an example of wanting to serve too many purposes with one assessment scheme. Built into the mandate were both continuous assessments to improve instruction and accountability to improve school outputs. I would argue that the main reason for the dramatic changes over a decade in the original assessment came about because persons focused on accountability and ignored the continuous assessment piece of the legislation. Innovative practices such as performance events and portfolios came under attack and were either eliminated or given reduced emphasis because of accusations that they were not technically strong enough as a basis for high-stakes school accountability. Although those features of the assessment were there for reasons of changing instruction, not accountability, the accountability tail wagged the good assessment dog and created confusion across the commonwealth. This is a good example of what I will discuss later. Assessments by themselves, no matter how high the stakes, are unlikely to produce the major changes in schools that are needed if there is to be increased student achievement. That is, focusing solely on outcomes is a big mistake!

Note

1. Several sources compile data about statewide assessments. The Educational Commission of the States (1997) produced a volume, *Education Accountability Systems in 50 States*, that showed 46 states having statewide assessments and 43 states having statewide standards, for example.

CHAPTER 2

Determining Purposes, Functions, and Targets
Reasons for Everything

W hy does one want to assess? Providing a rationale for an assessment is a logical place to begin. State assessments of the 1990s are couched in the language of school reform and justified by a focus on outcomes of schooling. Musick (1997) suggested that to focus on outcomes rather than inputs (e.g., facilities, materials) or processes (e.g., teaching methods) was a new and desirable development for those interested in reforming schools. He implied that if outcomes are specified, one need not worry about how they are accomplished.

Means, Ends, and Consistency

As you may suspect by now, I have a different view. Dewey (1916) told us that ends and means are inextricable. Some means are better than others as well. The choice of *means* influences the *ends* that will occur.

This is certainly the case when planning and implementing assessments. Increased test scores that result from students merely being more familiar with a test are not what is desired. What is desired is an increased performance that can be logically traced to either different or better inputs, processes, and schools experiences.

I believe an assessment should be consistent across the various dimensions of Figure 1.1 (see Chapter 1). Purposes and functions should be tied together logically and to each of the other categories of the grid.

Although I speak of purposes, one could just as easily speak of goals or aims of the assessment. There are, of course, ways to distinguish among purposes, aims, and goals. Yet, for the broad definition of assessment it is more important to have a rationale than it is to make pedantic distinctions among terms.

From purposes of the assessment to the structure of the assessment to what it emphasizes and how its results are reported, there should be a coherent rationale that can be communicated easily to the many audiences of large-scale assessment results. My assumption is that with such consistency one can make better sense of results, communicate more effectively with the many audiences for assessment results, and make more reasonable modifications or adjustments in the implementation of the assessment.

Purposes

I have labeled three general purposes for large-scale assessments: measure or increase academic achievement, provide accountability information, and, in a formative sense, improve instruction. A particular assessment may have one or more of these purposes, and the emphasis may be variously weighted across the purposes. One could define an assessment that only deals with achievement, but it would be difficult to have accountability as a major purpose without measuring achievement or other kinds of outcomes. It makes sense to wish to change instruction with an assessment, but it could be done without an accountability piece. That is, one could have an assessment that includes working with teachers to help them integrate assessment-type activities into a typical day of instruction.

NAEP cannot be reasonably expected to provide school accountability or directly improve instruction. It has no direct mechanism to change schools. It does, however, measure achievement and hopes to increase achievement nationwide by emphasizing standards and reporting long-term trends. The Kentucky assessment, however, places a premium on accountability through measures of achievement. It does little, if anything, to promote directly integrating assessment and instruction, or what was called the continuous assessment. I believe, however, that if it were consistent, it would spend more time and money giving that kind of training or producing conditions that produce the integration.

When defining the purposes of an assessment, it is desirable to follow the purposes to their logical and empirical conclusions. If, for example, one chooses a particular purpose (or purposes), it (or they) will have implications for other aspects of the assessment. If one wants to both measure achievement and change instruction, then implementing only an assessment is unlikely to produce the desired results. More reasonably, one should also try to change instruction directly. If, for example, one wishes teachers and schools to integrate more technology into instruction, then staff development programs should be instituted to provide the necessary training to create the opportunities for such change. Furthermore, the implementation of the new focus on technology should be directly evaluated just as its effects are being assessed in the formal assessment. For example, one might encourage the use of word processors in a writing assessment to facilitate the use of the technology.

One Purpose—One Assessment

Assessments should be tailored to serve very specific purposes. Expecting an assessment scheme to satisfy varying purposes is dangerous. Kentucky's assessment is an example of wanting to serve too many purposes with one assessment scheme. As I stated earlier, built into the mandate were both continuous assessments to improve instruction and accountability to improve school outputs. I would argue that the main reason for the dramatic changes taking place over a decade in the original assessment came about because persons focused on accountability and ignored the continuous assessment piece of the legislation. Had Kentucky chosen one assessment for one purpose, it would have saved itself time, money, and lots of hassle.

Functions

Hand in hand with questions of purpose are questions of function. Is the assessment designed to monitor, certify, evaluate, compare, or a combination of those functions? Again, I wish to mark on the grid the dominant function of the assessment. A high school leaving examination, such as that in Maryland, will rightfully focus on measuring achievement and function to certify students. By *certify* I mean some entity, usually a state department of education, is using a test to vouch for the competence of, again usually, its students.

States are also using assessment results to certify schools. Two examples are Virginia and Colorado, where performance on assessments and improved achievement are criteria for school accreditation. I include the accreditation process under the certification function.

A NAEP assessment functions mainly to monitor achievement in academic content areas and to trace patterns of achievement over time. My metaphor for an assessment that monitors is checking the oil in one's car. What is the level of the oil? I can push the metaphor a bit further by saying that the NAEP assessment also had an evaluation function because there are those who wish to say whether NAEP results are good enough. Is the oil level sufficiently high to be safe? A NAEP-type survey has no way to certify student competence or evaluate teachers and schools.

One could have a high school leaving examination that has two functions: certify students and evaluate schools. That is, the assessment could function both to certify students and, based on the proportions of students who pass the examination, evaluate the effectiveness of schools. Those with high pass rates would be evaluated positively; those with lower rates less so.

A problem with the above scenario is that the assessment may be at cross-purposes with broader outcomes of schooling. Schools do not only certify minimum competence. They provide advanced courses for college preparation, and they provide vocational training. Schools do a variety of things that are different from and not necessarily reflected by how many of their students pass a certification examination. Two schools with equal pass rates may have very different profiles on other outcomes. One, for example, may provide exemplary vocational training, and the other may provide major emphasis on advanced mathematics and science. Which is more effective? One may have eliminated physical education, music, and art in order to concentrate more on the basics; the other school may not. Which is more effective?

A second problem has to do with potential unexpected outcomes of an emphasis on a certification examination. The assessment could narrow the curriculum of the school, leading to less emphasis on equally desirable outcomes. A school may choose to reduce the time and effort it spends on one or more curricular areas because of the public pressure attached to its students' performance on the certification examination. It would not be a stretch of the imagination to have a school reduce its foreign language offerings to increase its emphasis on basic skills.

Another part of the assessment grid, reporting, may provide a solution to the above. (Again, it should be noted that I am emphasizing consistency across the grid.) Honest reports, emphasizing the limits of the assessment, may be used to inform persons about the difficulty of creating an assessment with two functions rather than one. It could report a variety of additional information about schools in addition to a passing rate. Still, it would be better, I believe, to stick with one primary purpose and leave it at that.

Formative and Summative Evaluation

I think it is important to distinguish between two types of evaluation: formative and summative (Scriven, 1967). An assessment combined with accountability, as is the Kentucky assessment, is using evaluation in a summative fashion. Assessment results are used to make judgments about the performance of schools with the purpose of providing rewards or sanctions. It is a summary judgment.

If there was no accountability attached to the assessment results, and the results were given back to schools so they could use them to improve what they were doing, then the evaluation would be formative. The question is whether assessment results are used to improve or make summary judgments about the target of the assessment.

I suppose an assessment could be both formative and summative. Yet, it would be better, I believe, to stick to one function just as it is better to stick to one purpose for an assessment.

Comparing

An assessment may have its function mainly to compare. I have in mind here the kinds of reports from TIMSS. To date, much of the reporting has focused on ranking countries according to their average scores and then making comparisons between countries. We know, for example, that the United States fares well in fourth-grade mathematics comparisons, is about average in the eighth grade, and is substantially below average in the last year of secondary school. Scores on the assessment are used to rank countries, or how they did in the international achievement Olympics, as they have been called.

The relationships between the purposes and functions are important to define. If, for example, one assesses achievement and merely wishes to monitor changes across time, it has implications (as will be discussed later), different from an assessment that wishes to include an accountability piece. Likewise, if an assessment wishes to both change instruction and measure achievement, implications for staff development are obvious. Knowing the purposes and functions should be the beginning of defining an assessment system.

From Whence the Rationale

Thinking clearly about a rationale for an assessment and its purposes and functions cannot be emphasized enough. While writing this, I kept thinking about what could be a good rationale for an assessment. I found contemporary discussions suspect both in terms of their reform rhetoric and their expectations. Likewise, I wonder about the excessive focus on what are arguably narrow outcomes.

What is the rationale for school reform that views assessments of outcomes as the driver of rapid change? One reads continually about how bad our schools are, but little to suggest the bases for the opinions; and, even if they are that bad, what view of schooling is it that expects dramatic improvement in short amounts of time?

I came up with two metaphors that do not work. One was a medical metaphor—a new drug to combat a new disease. The second was a factory operating at one half of its capacity. In both cases, one could expect dramatic changes if proper resources were devoted to inventing a new drug, increasing the skills of workers, or providing technology that was more modern and more efficient machinery for production. Notice that both metaphors depend on inputs and processes as well as outcomes to solve the apparent problems.

Are schools like medicine or factories? I think not. Especially when it comes to traditional outcomes of schooling—reading, writing, and arithmetic—I seriously doubt if there are new silver bullets or modern equipment that can produce dramatic changes in the short run. Rather, when it comes to schools, one has to be content with incremental changes over time that are the result of substantial changes in a school. Merely expecting consequences of assessment scores to change schools and schooling is not enough. There must be a concerted effort to change aspects of schools over time to provide changes in outcomes in the long run. I will deal with what I believe are desirable, big changes later.

Think of reading instruction. It has been a staple of elementary school instruction since there have been elementary schools. Think of the controversy between phonics and whole-language instruction for reading. Because reading is already a large part of the elementary school curriculum and there are arguments about the one best way to provide instruction in reading, what is the reform that will produce large reading gains quickly? Furthermore, is an expected outcome of phonics instruction the same as an expected outcome of whole-language instruction? Would an assessment that was fair to one approach be fair to the other? If one school was using phonics and another using whole-language, and one gave a whole-language assessment, what could be said about the two schools based on their scores on the assessment? Again, the issue is one of understanding the limits of what assessments can do and, through an emphasis on consistency, informing persons of both the strengths and weaknesses of an assessment along with the rationale that drives it.

Whoever said, "foolish consistency is the hobgoblin of small minds" was probably correct. Yet, consistency should be a major criterion for a good assessment. This means consistency of purpose, function, and all other categories of the grid.

Whatever the rationale, purposes, and functions of the assessment, it is important to be able to provide them to the varied audiences interested in education. A well-designed, consistent assessment, the components of which can be easily communicated, is the first step to a good assessment. Answering the questions I raised and dealing up front with these issues should give an assessment a firm foundation on which to deal with other crucial issues.

Measures

Does the assessment measure one thing or more? In general, national and international assessments such as NAEP (TIMSS is an exception, I believe) focus on one content area. State assessments vary greatly. When there is accountability, there are usually more measures. Again using Kentucky as an example, it measures several content areas and uses a weighted sum (composite or aggregate in the jargon of education) to come up with an overall score for a school. Most other state assessments also measure more than one content area.

Because schools are organized hierarchically, it is possible to summarize student achievement scores to get classroom, school, district, state, and even national measures. A number of assessments add to the achievement mix of other measures, usually at other levels in the hierarchy. Kentucky's accountability index includes composite student aggregate scores plus such school-level measures such as attendance rates, expectations for success, and successful transitions from school. (These additional measures are a small part of the accountability formula in terms of the weight attached to them and the actual weights they receive. Discussions of nominal weights, what I assign, versus real weights, what they actually become in a composite, can be found in most books on testing and assessment.) These measures also belong under the consistency category. Clear specifications of the purposes and functions of the evaluations should provide directions for the choice of measures.

Targets

Intimately tied to purposes and functions is the target, or targets, of the assessment. In general, the targets can be students or any structure in the educational hierarchy. Most state assessments first target students and then use student data for purposes of assessing classrooms, teachers, or schools. The TIMSS target is a student, but it uses national aggregates to make international comparisons. Tennessee's assessment uses student data aggregated to look at classrooms and teachers (Sanders, 1998). The Kentucky assessment uses summarized student data to reward or sanction schools.

Moving From Target to Target

As one moves from student data to aggregated data for classrooms, teachers, schools, states, or nations, new sets of questions about the assessment occur at every level. For example, an assessment focused on students needs to be justified in terms of the validity of the assessment to get good measures of student performance. An assessment that focuses on school-level results, however, can choose to measure students less well to save time and money. They can do this because a little bit of good information about each student does not tell one very much about the student, but it often gives a good overall picture of a school. Such assessments usually do some kind of sampling of students or items to make estimates of school performance (see the discussion about NAEP assessments and item sampling in Chapter 1). Depending on the level of aggregation, new questions emerge about the assessment and options for measurement become more evident. Again, the need for consistency is apparent.

Which Students?

A piece of the reform rhetoric includes what I consider the desirable notion that each child can learn and learn well. In the past, assessments excluded students with special needs without a lot of forethought. That day has passed. There are now big issues about how to accommodate students and what is a defensible rationale for either including or excluding them. If all students can learn then all can be tested.

Some accommodations are straightforward and noncontroversial. For instance, I have not heard anyone argue against allowing blind students to get a Braille version of the assessment. Other accommodations do create tension and debate: Should there be second-language versions of an assessment? Should one accommodate a nonreading student by reading the test aloud to get a measure of the student's comprehension?

Such issues must be addressed, and how they are resolved has important implications for results. In the most recent state NAEP reading assessment, several states made statistically significant gains between 1994 and 1998. In each of the states, a larger portion of students was excluded in 1998 than in 1994. This was because states were making more and different accommodations than were allowed in NAEP. So, the two groups of students represented different things in the two assessments. Are the scores comparable? Are the increases in performance because state educational reforms worked or because different types of students took part in the assessment?

Those last questions are not easily answered. It is hard to know what is a proper adjustment on the scores to make them comparable. One can be conservative and assume that students who were excluded would be among those with the lowest scores, and adjust accordingly. When that was done, each of the differences was estimated to be smaller than those that were originally reported.

Enabling Conditions

If one precisely pinpoints one target, there may be other targets that are necessary to hit in order to increase the likelihood of a successful intervention. Take again the example of the school-leaving examination. The major target for the assessment is, of course, a high school senior. So one could measure the student, decide whether a score reaches a minimal level, and leave it at that. Most programs of this sort do additional things, however. The most common maneuver is testing students prior to that year, often in the ninth grade, so they know where they stand and how much better they must do if they are to pass the examination. Exit examinations in Maryland do this and provide additional ways for students to gain experience so they have increased probabilities of passing by the time they are seniors. This is another example of how an assessment can be consistent across the areas shown in Figure 1.1. With fairness as a guide (I will talk more about this later), Maryland provides the opportunity for students to do well on the test by giving additional academic support. So, that very highly targeted examination turns out to have a number of other features. Those features include other targets and numerous support activities.

What Students, Grade Levels, and Schools?

For many assessments, the best answer to the question of who should one assess is *everyone*; but even this approach has problems. One of the problems is not, however, that there is a problem moving from level to level, making inferences about scores. In that scheme, one can get defensible scores at each level of the hierarchy: student, classroom, school, district, and so forth.

The problem, of course, is that such schemes are extremely costly. So, one has to make decisions about what levels to deal with. IEA sampled students in grade 8 and the last year of secondary school in several of its surveys. The rationale was that the eighth grade was the last year of compulsory schooling in a number of countries, so the surveys would reflect what all children experienced educationally in compulsory schooling. The end of secondary school was chosen to assess the best that a system did to educate its populace; that is, students in the last year of secondary school were getting the most, and perhaps the best, of what the system offered.

Kentucky initially assessed grades 4, 8, and 12 because they were the same grades as assessed by the NAEP. In addition, each of the grades could be used as a proxy for the whole school from which it came. This way, 4th-grade data were used for elementary school accountability, 8th-grade data for middle and junior high schools, and 12th-grade data for secondary school. The notion was that one could get both data comparable to national data and data for school accountability in one assessment.

The point of this is again a need for a rationale for doing things; reasons that can be conveyed to education's various audiences are keys to a successful assessment. One needs reasons for the choices and ways to make the reasons known.

Summary

This chapter is based on the notion that strong rationales are the foundations of good assessments. Those are the necessary, but not sufficient, conditions.

My notions include the following:

Good rationales lead to good assessment

One purpose for one assessment

Consistency across facets of the assessment is the be all and end all

Fairness should permeate the search for consistency

I operate under a firm belief that good early decisions about why to assess will provide a foundation for making consistent decisions as one proceeds through the assessment grid. The better one does in terms of providing a rationale for an assessment and the more clearly one can articulate its functions and purposes, the easier it will be to make decisions later. Such articulation should also help solve the problems of reporting results.

CHAPTER 3

Selecting the Frameworks, Standards, and Stakes for Assessments

In Chapter 2, I spoke about the need for logical consistency between the purposes, functions, targets, and other facets of an assessment. A similar kind of consistency between conceptual and technical aspects of a particular assessment is called, in the jargon of the day, alignment. Proper alignment implies that those who are being assessed (usually students) have experienced a common curriculum with common goals, the content of which is defined by a framework or content standards and sampled by test items.

Proficiency standards are set to define levels of performance on the assessment and typically have at least three such levels (e.g., less than adequate, adequate, and exemplary). As opposed to national tests such as the Scholastic Achievement Test (SAT) or the American College Test (ACT) that are related to no particular framework or curriculum, an alignment of a state assessment places a special premium on insuring equal opportunities for students to do well on their assessments.

Just as logical consistency is tricky business, so too is proper alignment. Frameworks are not impartial; inevitably, they are based on a point of view about what is important content and what are important processes. Writing items that sample fairly a framework is more art than science, and there is little in testing and assessment more controversial than standard setting. Notice I have said nothing about the stakes associated with an assessment. They merely make this above mix more muddled.

Sources for Content Standards

Before I get into my views on these matters, some sources should be useful to those who are implementing standards-based curricula and assessments.

Kendall and Marzano (1996) present content standards for kindergarten through grade 12 for a variety of subject matter areas. The Council of Chief State School Officers (CCSSO) produce each year a volume describing the status of state assessments, including a section about standards. Finally, Marzano and Kendall (1996) have a how-to-do-it book for creating standards-based curricula and assessments at the classroom, school, and district level.

Frameworks

Frameworks for tests, or similar organizational devices, have been a part of American education at least since Tyler's (1949) seminal curriculum book. Broader than a set of test specifications but narrower than a curriculum guide, a framework operates to provide one context for the assessment. The introduction to NAEP's history framework document gives five purposes for it:

> This document—which is the framework for the assessment—has been inspired by the best practice in schools. It has five purposes. First it provides background on NAEP and the development of this framework. Second, it defines a conceptual approach to U.S. history that incorporates a balanced treatment of America's common and diverse culture. Third, this document identifies content, ways of thinking and knowing about history, and skills that students at each grade level should master. Fourth, it describes desired characteristics of the assessment itself and recommends mixing knowledge and recall questions with more complex and thought-provoking questions. Finally, the framework presents preliminary descriptions of the three levels of achievement—basic, proficient, and advanced—by which performance will be reported. (NAGB, 1993a, p. 9)

The document contains a content matrix outline to guide the development of the assessment. Figure 3.1 is a replicate of the framework's Table 2.

Further specification of the framework comes from including defining questions for each theme. For example, Theme 2 includes such defining questions as the following:

> What have been the roles of men and women in American society (e.g., class structure, social mobility, social discrimination, family structure, neighborhood and community)? What common and diverse cultural traditions did Americans develop? How did Native Americans and other racial, ethnic, religious, and national groups contribute to the creation of a common culture in the United States as

Themes Periods	1. Change and Continuity in American Democracy: Ideas, Institutions, Practices, and Controversies	2. The Gathering and Interactions of Peoples, Cultures, and Ideas	3. Economic and Technological Changes and Their Relation to Society, Ideas, and the Environment	4. The Changing Role of America in the World
Three worlds and their meeting in the Americas (beginnings to 1607)				
Colonization, settlement, and communities (1607 to 1763)				
The Revolution and the new nation (1763 to 1815)				
Expansion and reform (1801 to 1861)				
Crisis of the Union: Civil War and Reconstruction (1850 to 1877)				
The development of modern America (1865 to 1920)				
Modern America and the World Wars (1914 to 1945)				
Contemporary America (1945 to present)				

Figure 3.1. NAEP History Framework

Kifer, E., *Large-Scale Assessments: Dimensions, Dilemmas, and Policy,* Copyright © 2001, Corwin Press, Inc.

well as to the development of distinct ethnic cultures? (NAGB, 1993a, p. 9)

Each cell of the table, defined by a particular theme and period and elaborated by the defining questions, is a source for issues addressed in the history assessment and for items to be written. The framework specifies the types of items or questions to be used. It mixes knowledge and recall questions with more complex and thought-provoking questions and provides a guide to the distribution of test questions across the content matrix.

I present this rather detailed description of the NAEP history framework to illustrate problems associated with the development of frameworks. I choose it not because it is a weak document. It would be easy to criticize bad work. To the contrary, the history framework is imaginative, thoughtful, and competent. What I hope is that, because it is good work, the issues I raise will be broadly applicable.

The question is not, therefore, whether the framework is any good. Rather, the question is what are the general issues associated with constructing content or assessment frameworks?

Consensus

Reading the history framework provides no clue about how controversial it might be. In fact, this history framework and the standards it defines is controversial (Diegmueller, 1994). Where one group sees balance, another sees political correctness. Controversies are not limited to history. Although the National Council of Teachers of Mathematics (NCTM; 1989, 1995) standards are reasonably well received, curricula based on its premises have been roundly criticized. Think, for instance, of the "fuzzy" mathematics debate in California or what has become almost an enduring dispute about the use of calculators on mathematics examinations. Frameworks incorporating NCTM standards are likely to be controversial, too.

One can cite other instances with other content areas as well. Reading, for instance, is controversial. It fares no better because the debate over whole-language instruction versus phonics has huge implications for building a framework and an assessment. Would a framework for a reading assessment for young students differ if it were based on phonics versus whole-language instruction? How would the test questions be different?

Process or Content

The difficulties are often centered on differences between those who are process oriented versus those who are content oriented. Should students be taught history or what historians do? What is the virtue of a mathematics curriculum that emphasizes solving problems more than correct calculations? Can one deal with the facts of history without discussing values related to the choice of facts? Should science be hands-on or are there certain basic notions about science that should be taught directly?

Those who design assessments must be ready to defend them. Each of the above issues is one that arises when building a framework. Part of the educational task of the designer is to convey to those who will be affected by the assessment some justifications for including and excluding content areas and processes.

Specification

Historically, NAEP has eschewed assessing any one particular curriculum. Until there are national curricula, then, NAEP will not be able to be aligned in the same sense that state assessments might be. That presents few, if any, problems when NAEP makes its national assessments. For state comparisons, however, the issue of alignment becomes critical. Performance in the different states is compared without noting the extent to which, if any, state frameworks are similar to the NAEP frameworks.

When one looks at the history framework, two major issues are apparent. First, the framework is extraordinarily broad. One cannot imagine a curriculum that could deal in depth with all of the issues suggested by the framework. It is a history version of what has been called the "mile wide and inch deep" phenomena (Schmidt et al., 1997). Although it is difficult to do so, a framework should help to focus assessments on fewer topics, but deal with them in greater depth.

Curricular Distinctions

The framework document for TIMSS makes crucial distinctions about curriculum. The writers distinguish between curricula that are intended, implemented, and achieved (Robitaille, 1993). The intended curriculum is that portrayed by documents such as a framework or curriculum guide, the implemented is that part of the curriculum the teachers teach, the achieved is that material students learn.

This is a serious question for the history framework. Because no curriculum could cover the history framework in depth, there is no way that one can bring the intended, implemented, and achieved curricula close together. The distinction helps one think about the importance of a framework that is doable not only in terms of dealing with it pedagogically but also being coherent enough for students to master it and for the public to understand.

The Questions

Accompanying the NAEP history framework document is an "Assessment and Exercise Report." The existence of the document suggests the difficulty of translating directly and unambiguously from a framework specification to a set of questions, test items, or other assessment entities.

Ideally, one would like a way to generate a set of test items that would both span and sample the domain of interest. In addition, it would be desirable if particular items were not dependent on who wrote them. The ideal is a machine that, given a set of specifications, spews out appropriate questions and covers an entire domain. One could then generate items at will and be confident of their measurement properties.

What is desirable is far from what is possible. Item writing is an art, not a science. Equally capable and knowledgeable persons will write very different questions based on the same framework or set of specifications. Because nuances in the items lead to unexpected responses, there are technical ways to go from what might be called a raw item set to one more polished. Large testing organizations typically have the means and experience to do this well. This allows them to know more about the responses they will get when an assessment is actually conducted.

Content Standards

Closely akin to frameworks are content standards. These, too, specify what students should know and be able to do, in the old NAEP phraseology. NCTM, I believe, developed the first set of content standards in 1989. Those standards defined the appropriate mathematical content—arithmetic, measurement, geometry, algebra, data analysis, and statistics—for different grade levels. They also specified desirable processes by arguing for a balance between computational competence and being able to solve mathematical problems. The standards are presently being revised. Other content disciplines (e.g., science) also have generated content standards. Each time NAEP conducts an assessment, it is dealing with content standards in some fashion.

There is no one way to generate content standards, nor are standards in the same content area similar across assessments. Adopting the NCTM standards does not necessarily lead to a common assessment. In fact, there are numerous Web sites (see Resource A) where it is possible to find out whether, for instance, a state has adopted a set of standards and what those standards are. The interested reader can then make comparisons between them. If you do that, you will find that standards-based educational reforms are notable for how they vary rather than how they are similar.

The problems of things being a "mile wide and inch deep" are endemic to content standards. Almost all are set through some kind of consensus procedure that tends toward defining more rather than less. Kentucky, for example, started with curriculum standards and has produced additional documents to be more specific about what will be assessed.

Twin goals of making standards deep, not wide, and narrow enough to be useful to teachers but broad enough to span important content dimensions are a continuing source of difficulty when defining content standards. States that have been doing standards-based assessments for a period of time have found that there is virtually always a need to revisit, rethink, and rewrite the standards.

Proficiency Standards

By *proficiency standards* I mean assigning labels to scores or performances that describe whether a student, for example, has mastered a particular content area. NAEP, which calls these *achievement levels*, was instrumental in producing and examining such proficiency standards (Phillips, 1996). Figure 3.2 depicts my fictitious version of NAEP achievement levels proficiency standards.

Notice that the three vertical lines (cut points on the score distribution in assessment jargon) divide the scores into the following four groups: below basic, at or above basic, at or above proficient, and at or above advanced. In this example, a small proportion of students is at or above advanced and a rather large proportion is below basic. In the NAEP history assessment, those proportions were 2% and 36%, respectively, for students in 4th grade. According to the NAGB (1993a), the achievement level definitions are as follows:

- **Basic:** Partial mastery of prerequisite knowledge and skills that are fundamental for proficient work at each grade.

- **Proficient:** Solid academic performance for each grade assessed. Students reaching this level have demonstrated competency over challenging subject matter, including subject-matter knowledge, application of such knowledge to real-world situations, and analytical skills appropriate to the subject matter.

- **Advanced:** Superior performance.

These definitions are constant across NAEP surveys. How they are arrived at varies from survey to survey, and the percentages of students at or above the proficiency levels varies from grade to grade and subject area to subject area.

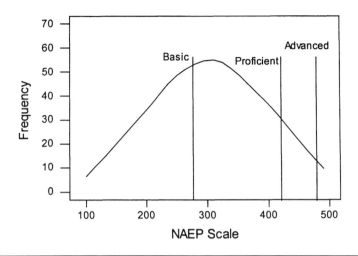

Figure 3.2. A Facsimile of NEAP Proficiency Standards

Setting Proficiency Standards

It is fair to say, I think, that NAGB pioneered achievement levels to better portray the achievements of U.S. students and simultaneously create expectations for higher performance. By taking test score interpretations out of a normative framework into a standards framework, one could talk about desirable levels of achievement. By *normative framework* I mean interpreting scores in terms of how well others in a group do. For example, if a score is at the 95th percentile, it indicates that only 5% of scores are above it. The problem is that with norm-based interpretations of scores there will always be a 95th percentile and, say, a third percentile; but, there is no way to know whether a score at the 95th percentile represents superior performance. It is just a score higher than most other scores.

Standards-based score interpretations do not depend on having properly defined norm groups. Scores are compared to the proficiency levels. A score is superior, basic, or advanced. The meaning of the score comes from an understanding of what proficiencies are needed to score at a particular level.

Using proficiency levels or standards allows one to create expectations of higher levels of achievement. A goal might be, for instance, to have all students reach a proficient level. That is a defensible goal. One cannot, however, have a goal that all students should score above the mean (a norm-based interpretation).

I wonder, however, if there has ever been a more controversial decision in the history of NAEP. From the beginning, the process of setting achievement levels was criticized (National Academy of Education, 1993), and the criticisms have continued with other evaluations, the latest of which was conducted by the National Academy of Science (Pellegrino, Jones, & Mitchell, 1998).

The process of setting proficiency or achievement standards would appear to be straightforward. Nothing could be further from the truth. Although there are many methods used to set the levels (Jaeger, Mullis, Bourque, & Shakrani, 1996), there is no way to escape that they are essentially judgmental. No matter how one sets the levels, they are arbitrary. Because they are arbitrary, there is no defensible way to know what is being referenced in terms of the content being measured and no way to know how high or low the standards are. Use two different methods to set standards and get two different results. A common method used by two groups of persons yields different results. Different methods and different groups yield still different results.

Item Difficulty Versus Cognitive Complexity

Another reason it is hard to reference proficiency standards is that many standard-setting methods are based on *item difficulty*, the technical term for the proportion of students who answer a given item correctly. That technical property of a test question is not the same as the conceptual complexity implied by answering an item correctly. A question such as, "Give me the names of the persons who came over on the Mayflower," could be very difficult (in the item-difficulty sense), but it is cognitively simple. One could memorize a list and simply recall them. Suppose I asked, however, "Which way would you turn to head toward Los Angeles if you were going north in St. Louis?" A correct answer to this question requires rather complex understandings. Nevertheless, it would likely be an easy question. Standards set on item difficulty are often interpreted in terms of cognitive complexity. Because there is not a one-to-one correspondence between item difficulty and cognitive complexity, score interpretations get confused.

Theoretically, the answer to defining proficiency standards well is to have well-specified domains of knowledge and tight links between that domain and item writing and standard setting. The *New Standards Project* (Resnick et al., 1995) has attempted to create such tightly defined assessment tools.

How such tightly defined assessments relate to instruction is one final complication associated with proficiency standards. Something taught well may appear to be easy, but something that is easy if not taught or not taught well may appear to be difficult. That means that standards and instruction must be tightly coupled if score interpretations are to be defensible.

Opportunity-to-Learn Standards

OTL began with IEA studies. In that context, it was a measure of the implemented curriculum through ratings by teachers. Porter (1995) has extended those notions and has argued for broader conceptions of OTL. Although not so thoroughly discussed or embraced in the standards-based literature, OTL is, in my mind, a crucial component of any assessment. (OTL standards, it should be noted, are voluntary ones in Goals 2000.) The logical consistency that is desirable among components of the assessment should extend to whether students, or in fact teachers, have had opportunities to be successful on measures to which they are exposed.

Figure 3.3 points out the power of the OTL. It shows boxplots of teacher ratings of OTL for four different mathematics types in the SIMS. These come from a chapter having to do with participation in mathematics (Kifer, 1994). Boxplots or box-and-whisker plots are easily understood. The line that separates the box into parts is the median score, a center of the distribution. The top of the box is the 75th percentile; the bottom is the 25th. Therefore, the boxes contain 50% of the data and show the spread of the middle part of the data. The whiskers cover about 95% of the data. Outliers, odd data points outside the whiskers, are marked with an asterisk. Boxplots allow the eye to see whether centers and spreads of distributions are similar or different.

According to teachers, students in algebra classes are exposed to much more material on the test than students in other classes. Look, for example, at the algebra content area. Students in algebra classes, with the exception of some noticeable outliers, had an opportunity to learn virtually the whole test. Although there is variation within the other class types, no other class type begins to have the coverage afforded students in algebra classes. Westbury (1992) discussed the advantages of being placed in an algebra class and its curricular implications. Students in those grade 8 classes performed just as well as Japanese students in the SIMS.

There are those who would argue that Westbury's (1992) findings were the results of high-ability students being placed in algebra classes. That is not necessarily the case. I found that U.S. students who were in the top 10% of the pretest distribution had a 50/50 chance of being placed in eighth-grade algebra (Kifer, 1994). That is, there are as many talented students not receiving the best curricula as there are receiving it.

OTL has different implications depending on the context of the assessment. OTL is especially appropriate when one deals with so-called "high stakes" assessments, a topic I turn to next. Fairness dictates that students who are to be assessed should have the opportunity to learn what will be assessed.

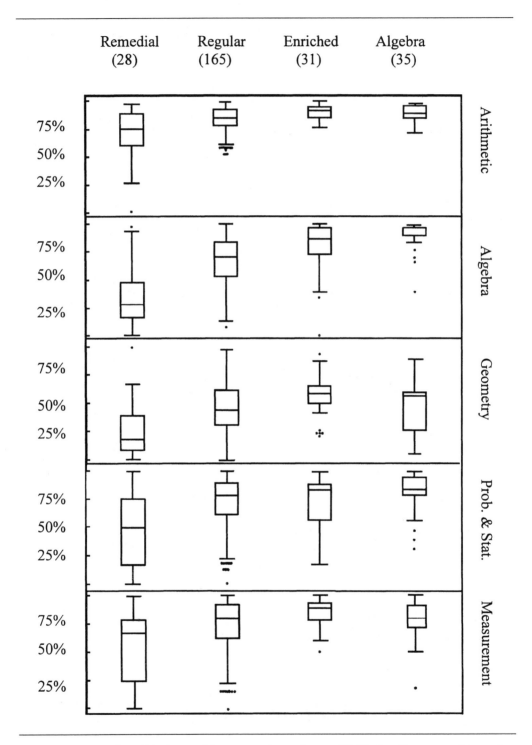

Figure 3.3. Teachers' Ratings of Opportunity to Learn (OTL) for Classroom Types by Content Area

Assessment Standards

Most large-scale assessments do not make explicit commitments to assessment standards. Most, however, attempt to adhere to good assessment practices.

There are several sources detailing such practices. NCTM has published their evaluation standards that contain principles related to general assessment, student assessment, and program evaluation. There are 14 standards that emphasize evaluation and assessment and feature what NCTM (1989, 1995) describes as areas of "increased attention" and "decreased attention." Examples of things that need increased attention are assessing how students think mathematically and integrating assessment and instruction. Examples of things that should receive decreased attention are assessing what students do not know and measuring isolated bits of mathematics.

A second source for assessment standards is the *Standards for Educational and Psychological Testing* (1997) developed jointly by the American Psychology Association and the National Council on Measurement in Education. The standards address such issues as constructing tests, using tests properly, the rights of test takers, and testing minorities. This new version includes material directly related to large-scale assessments.

Finally, one can also turn to *The Program Evaluation Standards: How to Assess Evaluations of Educational Programs* (Joint Committee on Standards for Educational Evaluation, 1994) for additional information when evaluation is a focus. These standards are a revised version of those produced in the early 1980s and include standards dealing with the utility, feasibility, propriety, and accuracy of evaluations. Familiarity with these sources is a necessity for those involved in creating, implementing, and interpreting large-scale assessments. Even a cursory look at the standards would show that far too often our assessments do not reach the technical desirability described in the above.

Stakes

Central to the marriage of standards-based assessment and educational reform is the notion that if consequences are attached to the assessments, good assessments will change schools and increase student achievement.

That tests influence what is done in schools is not a new notion. In fact, Madeus and O'Dwyer (1999) suggested that "the power of an examination to shape what was taught and learned was noted at least as far back as the 16th century" (p. 688). Accountability through assessments has been justified in a variety of ways. Resnick and Resnick (1992) said, "You get what you assess; you do not get what you do not assess; and, build assessments toward which you want educators to teach" (p. 82). Conversely, Stake (1999, p. 669) cites the following negative consequences:

Instruction is diverted.

Student self-esteem is eroded.

Teachers are intimidated.

The locus of control of education becomes more centralized.

Undue stigma is affixed to the school.

School people are lured toward falsification of scores.

Some blame for poor instruction is redirected toward students when it should rest with the profession and the authorities.

The withholding of needed funding for education appears warranted.

Levels of Consequences

My assessment grid contains three general entries: high, moderate, and low. In terms that would not be funny to students, for *high* stakes they would be told that their whole future depended on the results of the assessment. *Moderate* stakes would have some direct influence on their future, perhaps something such as the results of an in-class, teacher-constructed test. *Low* stakes would be a matter where students might choose to be indifferent to the outcomes, and that, of course, would depend on how a student views a test. I doubt that there is such a thing as a no-stakes exam. Students are likely to have enough experience taking tests that they feel some sense of obligation to take them somewhat seriously regardless of the circumstances.

High-Stakes Assessments

A rationale for attaching severe consequences to the outcomes of assessment is much like Dr. Samuel Johnson's defense of hanging: "Depend upon it, Sir, when a man knows he is to be hanged in a fortnight, it concentrates his mind wonderfully" (Boswell, 1922, p. 257). High-stakes assessments are meant to focus the attention of the educational community on improvement.

High Stakes: Whom and What

High stakes logically can be attached to each level of an educational hierarchy: students, teachers or classrooms, schools, districts, states, and even nations. To be high stakes, the assessment must have serious consequences for its target. In the Kentucky assessment, the stakes are mainly at the school level and the consequences are rewards and sanctions. Teachers in schools that improve over time receive generous cash bonuses. Schools that do not improve are potentially subject to an array of negative consequences, including a sanction that calls for the commonwealth to take control of the poor performance school. (More than one critic of Kentucky's accountability system has suggested that, in fact, it may be the schools that do not improve that should be getting additional resources.) In something such as the Maryland high school exit examination or the New York State Regents examination, the stakes are mainly for students with a high school diploma or a particular kind of course credit on the line.

However, it is difficult to imagine high stakes at the national level. Goals 2000 stated that the United States was to be first in the world in mathematics and science by the year 2000. That is an outcome without a way to attach consequences to it. If there were a direct way to reward or punish the educational system for not meeting the goal, that would indeed be a high-stakes assessment.

Unintended Consequences of High-Stakes Assessments

Despite what appears to be the popularity of attaching stakes to assessments, the process is not without its weaknesses (Linn, 1998a, 1998b; Linn & Herman, 1997). There are unintended consequences, both positive and negative, associated with high-stakes testing. The Kentucky high-stakes assessment is a case in point. It was a part of a broader set of school reform measures that included reforms in finance, elementary schooling, teacher certification, and new programs to extend the influence of schools. It brought national attention to Kentucky and its innovative approaches to assessing students, something Kentuckians viewed in positive terms. On the other hand, the assessment was the lightning rod of the reform. Criticism of the reform focused on the perceived limitations of the assessment. The reform was perceived to be not going well because the assessment was not reliable and valid. Portfolio assessment and performance events, instituted as a way to change instruction, were criticized for being not sufficiently reliable to be a part of the accountability system. Such confusion among purposes in a high-stakes environment led to the elimination of performance events, an assessment approach that enjoyed remarkable esteem among those who knew most about them. They were examples of "tests worth teaching to" and these showed potential to change instruction.

The Kentucky assessment was changed dramatically in a rather short period of time despite evidence that initially some features of it were producing desirable changes in instruction. The high-stakes accountability led to the demise of first-rate assessment. All this despite evidence that most facets of the reform, especially the financial ones, were quite successful.

Just as a spotlight focuses attention on one part of the stage, so too high-stakes assessments focus on one part of schooling. When there is consistency between standards, items, rubrics, proficiencies, and stakes, there is also a narrowing of the focus of the schools, and that is not only in the sense of narrowing the academic outcomes, something that could be considered okay by those who want curricula that are narrower and deeper. If there is an influence of the assessment on curriculum, then those subject areas and grade levels that are targets will likely get the lion's share of the attention in what is reformed or changed. Those not assessed, although arguably important, will get much less attention; and there are other outcomes of public schooling, for example, those associated with being a good citizen, that are as important or more important than academic outcomes. Those, too, get short shrift.

Stakes for Whom

If the stakes are not consistent, another set of problems ensues. Again, Kentucky is a good example. The assessment was high stakes for schools (teachers), but low stakes for students. If students did not perform well because they did not take the assessment seriously enough, the school could be punished. There were no direct consequences of student performance so there was a problem, some persons maintained, motivating the students to do well. One perhaps apocryphal story was that students in a Kentucky high school threatened to not do well on the assessment unless school personnel agreed to remove the speed bumps in the student parking lots.

The question of motivating students created murkiness for teachers in Kentucky between what was considered allowable assistance versus questionable practices during the assessment. There were numerous instances of alleged cheating by teachers who directly or indirectly aided students. None of these things would likely have happened if the high stakes (i.e., rewards and sanctions) were not a part of the assessment.

Moderate-Stakes Assessments

When an assessment publishes results and makes comparisons between its targets, I think of that as setting moderate stakes. The public is told who or what is doing well and not doing well. Reports take the form of report cards, ranking schools and districts, and other means to give consumers information about students, teachers, or schools.

A good report card displaying many facets of a school's performance is, I believe, a desirable way to inform the public how well a school is doing and it attaches consequences to the assessment. There are numerous examples of innovative reporting, several of which have been published by Goals 2000 and can be found on their Web page.

Low-Stakes Assessments

Those who develop NAEP assessments worry about their stakes being too low. Students may not be motivated to perform as well as they can. Those concerns are what one finds with a low-stakes assessment. Students may receive nothing by their participation in NAEP and therefore may not be interested in doing well on the assessment.

Suppose students were highly motivated to take NAEP assessments. How much better might they do? This question is raised when there are few, if any, consequences for students to do well. Results of NAEP assessments might be higher if there were higher stakes attached to the assessment or if students saw direct consequences of the results of their work on the tests.

Deciding on Stakes

A colleague of mine loves to talk, not positively, about education initiatives that turn opportunities into ultimatums. Secondary schooling in the United States was an opportunity at the turn of the century when only about 5% of a cohort got a degree. It is now an ultimatum. There is little doubt that high stakes produce ultimatums. Are things so bad that we need more threats?

I am convinced that the negative consequences of high-stakes assessments are greater than the positive ones. I believe that we should look for carrots, not sticks, when looking at the consequences of an assessment system.

As I write, the state of Idaho has an assessment initiative that illustrates what I think is an important issue in choosing the stakes of an assessment. Should the stakes be carrots or sticks? The state is going to develop a high school exit examination. They could make it high stakes by creating an examination that certified competence without which a student would not receive a high school diploma. Another possibility, however, capitalizes on the fact that Idaho school districts, not the state, now award high school diplomas. So, Idaho could choose to make its exit examination an opportunity for a student to get a state diploma in addition to the district diploma. By doing so, the assessment is no longer high stakes. If the stakes were lowered, I would not expect it to produce the unintended negative consequences of a high-stakes assessment. Idaho can get additional benefit from the lower or moderate stakes, too. I will write about this later when I discuss outcomes. For now, however, it would be possible to make the state diploma an opportunity rather than an ultimatum. I think that would be a good thing to do.

A Short Confession

In general, I like assessments without high stakes attached to them. I believe the unintended negative consequences of rewards and sanctions attached to assessments are more potent than the positive consequences. They do more harm than good in the sense of corrupting good assessment practices.

On the other hand, it may be possible to design an assessment with high stakes that were not a corrupting influence. The problem is we know little about how particular consequences influence different assessment audiences. A student may take an advanced placement examination with the view that it matters little or matters a lot whether the score gets college credit. Teachers in a school may be influenced differently by one kind of consequence versus another. There is much to be known in the stakes arena about the relationship between consequences, the perceptions of various audiences of those consequences, and what might happen in a similar setting without well-specified consequences. Some persons like to take tests, believe it or not!

CHAPTER 4

Outcomes and Assessments

Outcomes

By their nature assessments deal with outcomes, so this is an odd name for a major section of the assessment grid. I could find no better to distinguish two very different approaches to assessment results. I call them status versus growth or change outcomes.

By *status*, I mean assessment outcomes gathered at one time that provide estimates, for example, of what a student knows. Examinations such as the SAT, ACT, bar examination, and assessments such as high school exit examinations are status measures because their purpose is to affix a score that purports to reflect a person's knowledge or ability at that time.

Change or growth measures seek to monitor differences in achievement over time and, when focused on students, describe what has been learned. NAEP's long-term trend assessments do just that. They trace mathematics achievement over almost 30 years. Other assessments focus on differences and expect improvement over time. For example, the accountability system in Kentucky is based on improvement over 2 school years. It is not the students in Kentucky but the schools that are expected to change positively: Those that do get rewarded; those that do not get sanctioned.

Cohort or Longitudinal Change

Assessments focused on change or improvement can measure those differences in two primary ways. Suppose the target is students. The assessment can measure the same students at two or more different times or they can measure different students over two or more occasions. The first way, the longitudinal one, follows students through their school career. How did they perform, say, in first grade versus how are they performing in fifth grade? The method ascertains how much a student learned in a given amount of time.

(Those measures could, of course, be aggregated to the classroom or school level to estimate how much growth occurred in those contexts.)

The second approach, measuring cohorts, gathers information, for instance, on fifth graders on two different occasions. The students measured at Time 1 are different from those measured at Time 2; but, the grade level or cohort (in this example, fifth grade) remains the same so one can construe the measurement as focusing on change or growth, although not in a true longitudinal fashion.

The Tennessee assessment is a good example of a longitudinal assessment (Sanders, 1998; Sanders, Saxton, & Horn, 1997). Students are measured in each grade level each year. Differences between achievements for the first year and second year are computed for students, classrooms/teachers, and schools. These results describe changing performance over time based on measurements taken of the same individuals.

The Kentucky assessment makes cohort comparisons at the school level. For example, students in fourth grade are measured each year. The differences between test scores of students who form a baseline are compared to test scores of students 2 years later. Note that the comparison is between fourth-grade scores based on the accomplishments of different students—hence, it is a cohort comparison. Students who formed the baseline are, say, now in sixth grade but their scores are not compared to what they received in fourth grade.

Which Type of Outcome

Whether an assessment measures status or some form of improvement depends on the purpose and function of the assessment. Assessments to certify, whether they are high school completion examinations or the bar examination, focus on status measures. So, too, for surveys such as NAEP or TIMSS where the purpose is to evaluate or compare outcomes at one time point. (There are, of course, exceptions to that. NAEP produces trend surveys and SIMS was a true longitudinal study for eight educational systems).

Some form of surveying focused on change or growth is appropriate when the purpose is to monitor or evaluate a set of persons or things over time. If the emphasis is on change, growth, or reform, that suggests the need for either longitudinal or cohort designs.

Cohort or Longitudinal

Neither a cohort nor a longitudinal design is best for all purposes. Persons in the schools know the major weakness of a cohort design. Cohorts change. I remember a teacher in my son's high school talking about the senior class that year. The class had won all sorts of state and national honors in academic areas, scholarships, school government, debate, band, soccer, drama, and others I am forgetting. As she was marveling over their accomplishments, she abruptly changed course and said, "but those juniors."

Persons who deal with databases know the difficulty of longitudinal data: keeping track! There is a substantial amount of mobility in the schools. Students move from class to class, school to school, in state and out, and so on. Without careful tracking, a longitudinal study can easily be invalidated by huge numbers of dropouts from the sample. Also, the degree of mobility influences how well one estimates the effects of classrooms or schools.

Student mobility is an issue in a number of different ways. Mobility rates (students moving in and out) vary from classroom to classroom, school to school, and district to district within states. When there are stakes attached to the assessment, a decision has to be made about whom is responsible for the mobile student. How long must a student be in a classroom or school before that teacher or school should be held accountable for the student's performance?

As is the case for many of these issues, choices about the form of the outcomes depend on the clarity and coherence of the assessment. Even when the choice of type of outcome is clear, there remain technical issues, such as mobility, to resolve.

Assessments

What form should the assessment take? Should it be multiple-choice or some form of performance assessment? Should it be a combination? Why or why not?

We know lots about multiple-choice examinations, much less about the various forms of performance assessment. Neither form is perfect. One could say that multiple-choice exams are old and wrong; performance assessments are new and wrong.

There are two main arguments I believe for using multiple-choice examinations. One is efficiency. Because we know a lot about them, they are easier to generate, score, and report. They also cost less than performance assessments. Because they are perceived to measure particular pieces of what we aim to measure (in the jargon of testing, they measure facets of the domain of interest), they can be constructed to cover more and broader content. Perhaps they were invented because our curricula are broad, not deep.

If ease and coverage are the strengths of multiple-choice examinations, the realistic nature (authenticity and genuineness in educational jargon) of performance assessments is their strength. A writing portfolio is preferable to a multiple-choice writing test, which typically is an editing test, because the nature of the task corresponds closely with what one does in real life.

Performance assessments have in common that they can demand reasons and justifications as well as answers to questions. Whether the form be an open-ended question (constructed response), a performance event (a task such as a science experiment often done jointly), an essay (writing on demand), or a collection of student work (portfolio), the tasks are structured so as to demand not only knowledge about something but also reasoning about it.

Although arguments are made about multiple-choice items being able to measure "higher order" thinking (jargon for responses to questions that are not simply based on recalling something), there is no way that a multiple-choice item can capture how a student reasons. That, by definition, must be gotten outside of giving the student answers to choose from. Reasoning about something needs the *something* but that is all.

Standardized tests containing multiple-choice questions often include a set of norms so a score on the test can be compared with other scores. One can say how a student compares with all other students or how a state average compares with a national average. Performance measures are beginning to appear in standardized form and do now have national norms, but those are not so extensive as those found with multiple-choice examinations.

Because part of the rationale for large-scale assessments is to make them standards based, I find myself not overly concerned about whether there are national norms. If the assessment is linked to the standards and standards are well articulated, then one can draw inferences about the meaning of the scores without needing a national comparison. If fact, a major justification for standards-based reporting was to eliminate the necessity for norm-based comparisons. It should be pointed out that the public seems not to share my opinion. I discuss that issue later in the book.

I do not give multiple-choice tests in my classes. On purely pedagogical grounds, I believe performance assessments are superior. If one wants to change instruction in the direction of students being able to solve problems and provide reasons, the assessment choice is clear: One should use performance measures. If there are other purposes (e.g., editing is considered important in its own right, not in the context of one's writing) that lend themselves to multiple-choice items, I question the purposes.

A Technical Note

Whether the intent is to assess status (i.e., what is known) or growth (i.e., what is learned), almost all assessments must deal with comparability of the measures over time. The College Board, for example, equates the SAT from year to year so the scores will hypothetically be comparable. A verbal score of 550 is to mean the same thing regardless of the year the test was taken.

The issue of comparability is by no means simple. This is especially true when dealing with assessments where growth is presumed to occur over time. How does one know that the differences reflect true change or differences between tests that were given? Even worse, if it is a cohort design, differences between the cohorts are additional sources of variation that might make it appear as though there has been growth when, indeed, there has not been any.

Another issue is that of test and test-question security versus distributing them so students and teachers know better what is contained in an assessment. Keeping items secure helps the equating process. It also tends to reduce costs because new items do not have to be developed each testing cycle. However, keeping items secure makes the test less useful in the sense of providing good information to test takers.

Keeping tests comparable over time is extremely complex and requires fancy technical models. Fortunately, I do not have to deal with them in this book. There are a number of books that discuss such technical matters, among them Frederiksen, Mislevy, and Bejar (1993).

Technology, Support, and Reporting

Technology

There are at least two ways that using technology becomes an issue for large-scale assessments. The first and most important is the question of whether new technologies should be part of what students should be able to do effectively. That is, should they be a part of the assessment framework or content standards? The prevailing view, I believe, is strongly in favor of using technology in schools and enhancing the capacities of students to use it well.

The second issue is whether students should be able to use technology when taking the assessments themselves. If there is to be consistency across the assessment grid, then the answer is clear. Students should use the technologies during the test if they use technology during instruction.

Calculators or Computers

There are few issues so contentious as the use of calculators on mathematics assessments. I listened to discussions during the public hearings for the Voluntary National Test where one esteemed mathematician said that students should never use calculators, and another esteemed mathematician said students should be encouraged to use calculators virtually all the time.

In addition to personal preferences about the use of calculators, there is also a set of fairness issues. If students are in mathematics classes where technology is thoroughly integrated, they are likely to be penalized if they do not have access to what they normally use. But, such students may be advantaged on the test if they have access to powerful tools that are not available, say, to students in other classrooms or schools. If there is no consistency between what students typically experience in the classroom and what they are allowed to do in an assessment, there are serious questions raised about the validity of the assessment.

NAEP allows, for example, calculator use on some forms (but not others) and hands out the calculators that will be used. When mathematics portfolios are part of an assessment, students typically use calculators as much as they desire.

The issue of whether to use calculators is a question, again, of consistency. If their use is advocated for instruction, they should be used in the assessment. If there are goals about increasing the use of technology, then technology should be used in the assessment.

My experience is that the desire to have these issues settled in some logical, consistent way is very optimistic. Too many persons have too many strong opinions on these issues. Nevertheless, a decision has to be made about whether students use calculators and under what conditions they are used.

Word Processors

The use of word processors when writing on-demand essays is equally problematic. There is evidence to suggest that when students are taught writing while using word processors and not allowed to use them in an assessment, their writing scores are severely and negatively affected. Russell and Haney (1997) conducted an experiment about the use of word processors. (Experiments in education are difficult to do and typically not found in the research literature. Results from a true experiment seem to me to carry more weight than those of a more typical correlational study.) They wanted to see the effects on writing of students who were instructed with word processors but were not allowed to use them for the assessment. Across the board, regardless of the criteria, performance without word processors was worse. Russell (1998) replicated those findings.

It seems clear to me that students taught with word processors should be able to use them in the assessment setting. How else are they to be able to show the best they can do? Nevertheless, decisions have to be made about whether the assessment will be consistent with instruction.

Adaptive Devices or Accommodations

There is a consensus that assessments should be given to as many students as possible. There is also, I believe, a consensus that accommodations should be made. Where there is not a consensus, as alluded to earlier, there is the question of how many and what kinds of accommodations are appropriate.

The evidence is clear that students do better when they have appropriate adaptive tools during the assessment. Do these tools invalidate their scores? That is the question and one that has to be answered.

It should be pointed out that there is no legal basis for excluding accommodations when a test has serious consequences. The Americans with Disabilities Act of 1990 requires that disabled students be provided with reasonable accommodations.

Support

I had a difficult time coming up with the label for this part of the grid. By *support* I mean providing additional assistance to persons who are affected by an assessment. I mean additional resources and time should be provided to all those who feel the impact of the assessment.

Depending on the nature of the assessment, its purposes and functions, there may be a need for such support mechanisms. The support can be given to students, teachers, administrators, or any combination of them. But, if the assessment requires special things for any of those involved, they should be given access to special training.

Students

For example, if the assessment functions to certify levels of competence of students, both prudence and fairness dictate providing special services to students. If, for example, the assessment can be construed to be unfair to a particular class of students or students did not have the opportunity to learn material that is contained in the assessment, there are potential legal consequences. *Debra P. v. Turlington* (1981), a now-famous Florida court case, argued that minority students did not have the opportunity to learn the materials on a certification examination. Therefore, their scores were not valid.

There is, of course, a reason to provide support and assistance despite the threat of a lawsuit. It is the right thing to do. Kentucky's reform included not only a high-stakes assessment but also a variety of additional services for students. These extended school services could include after-school tutoring, Saturday tutoring, or free summer school enrollment. In addition, Kentucky provided a variety of services through what were called Family Resource Centers, organizations attached to low-income schools to provide both educational and social services.

Teachers

If the purpose of the assessment is to change instruction, then teachers should be provided access to the knowledge and granted time to learn the new methods. I said earlier how flimsy I thought the notion was that if one imposed a set of educational outcomes, it would be clear how one should go about meeting them. I believe that processes and outcomes are thoroughly intertwined. If one wants to influence instruction in a particular way, then it is necessary to provide directly the experiences that teachers need. One reason, I believe, that Kentucky's assessment had to be changed so dramatically is that it did not provide the kinds of staff development that teachers needed. There is a touch of irony here. Although Kentucky's assessment did not certify students, it provided services for them. With high-stakes accountability for schools and the direct pressure on teachers, it did not provide adequate services for them. Again, the need for consistency is apparent.

Staff

Someone in each school needs to have intimate knowledge of the properties of the assessment. In Kentucky, a new class of administrators and district and school assessment coordinators emerged to deal with the complexities of the assessment. Regardless of who is trained, some provision needs to be made to train persons well to provide information and guidance about the assessment.

The issues dealing with teachers and staff fall under the broad rubric of professional development. There are new ideas and practices in professional development that should be adopted. The interested reader is directed to the work of Guskey and Huberman (1995).

Reporting

Regardless of the purposes and functions of an assessment, effectively reporting results is a necessity. Who gets the reports, what information they receive, and how it is presented is crucial.

Students and Parents

The first audience for most test score results is the test taker. If a person is either willing or demanding to take a test, he or she should find out what are the results. How to report and what to report is an art. The National Goals Panel (1998, 1999) has some exemplary reports and practices from different states. The reports are imaginative, informative, and notable for their variety. Clearly there has been some thinking done about how and what to report.

The Voluntary National Test planned to set a precedent for reporting to students, parents, and the public by releasing tests immediately after they were taken nationally. Not only would the test questions and correct answers be made public but also individual reports to students and parents would include question-by-question responses of the student compared with correct answers and what were considered exemplary answers on constructed re-sponse items. This represents a huge step in making available useful informa-tion to those who take the tests.

In most cases—think of the SAT or most state testing programs—students do not get such detailed information about their performance, and what is provided is not provided very quickly. This is the case despite the evidence of the power of formative testing to improve the student's achievement. With what is now becoming within schools almost universal access to the Internet and computing networks, the technology to produce complete and immedi-ate results of testing is now available. With imagination, that medium may change how we think of reporting test score information not only to students but teachers and parents as well.

Class/Teacher

If a purpose of the assessment is to change classroom instruction or if the as-sessment is formative, then useful reports to teachers are important. The power of formative tests is well documented (Bloom, 1968). So, it follows that teachers need reports that they can use to judge what they are doing well and what they are doing not so well. Typically, question-level information contain-ing student responses can be very helpful to teachers. Note, however, that in assessments where security of the assessment is a major issue, it may be diffi-cult to provide the kinds of reports that are most useful.

The goal of these reports is to allow teachers to adjust their instruction so that weaknesses are strengthened. Detailed information informatively pre-sented is essential to perform that function, but that is not enough. The com-plexity of most assessments means that time and money must be spent to make sure that the information teachers receive is understandable and understood.

School or District

As one moves up the educational hierarchy, there are different information needs. Schools need classroom information; districts need school informa-tion. What to provide and how to provide it are crucial here, too. A number of examples of these kinds of reports can be found on the Internet. In Resource A, I list Internet sites I found particularly useful when writing this. Looking at state department sites and noticing what is being done will reward the con-summate surfer. There are good examples out there.

Public

State assessments, for the most part, are controversial. They tend also to be very complex. Controversial, complex things are not easily communicated. Yet, the success of the assessment may depend on how the public is informed.

First the legislators and elected officials. I include in the *public* elected officials who propose the ideas and legislators who pass the statutes leading to statewide assessments. This is a particularly difficult audience because they deal with assessment issues at an abstract level. To propose is not to do. To legislate is not to implement. To implement is to get one's hands dirty. Neither entity is interested in that.

There appear to be inordinate pressures on elected officials and legislators to implement assessments as a part of reforming schools. It is difficult to argue against standards (although I try a little later in the book) and, given legislative penchants, not to want higher ones than the next state's. These pressures are forced on persons who typically know little about assessments and are faced with conflicting views about the efficacy of any one set of approaches to assessing students, teachers, or schools.

My answer to the general problem is more knowledge and better information. It is important that those who propose and those who legislate these assessments get information about the potential consequences of their actions. If I were an elected official, I would go beyond the typical expert testimony to get my information. I would go back to my constituents, especially those who will be most affected by the assessments—teachers and students. I would try to find the squeaky wheels and the most highly opinionated persons so I got the full range of views before I voted to assess anything.

The other public. Assessments contain language that means something to experts, but may mean little to reporters or lay persons. Look across the grid and notice the words we think we understand that either make no sense or have a commonsense meaning different from the way it is used. To a person outside the assessment arena, the precision of our language is just jargon. Everyone believes in accountability, but perhaps not the one we believe in. What are stakes and what makes them high or low? What is a cohort, performance event, constructed response, or portfolio? What is a proficiency standard, content standard, framework, or opportunity to learn? The trick is to convey to the public what is done, what is found, and why each is important. This is a difficult task.

I believe, however, that it is as important to produce information about the rationale and purposes of assessment as it is to report assessment results. Convincing the public of the power of any particular assessment schema depends as much on public understanding as it does on higher test scores. Higher test scores mean little if one cannot understand what they mean and how they reflect what is being done or done better in the school setting.

Technology

One last time! The power of computing and the Internet have not been used in reporting. I mentioned the NAEP CD-ROM as an example of what can be done in the computing arena. Likewise, I mentioned what proponents of the Voluntary National Test envisaged for reporting results via the Internet. More and better use of these vehicles is a necessity. Imaginative use of this technology is the next step for better reporting and better information.

CHAPTER 5

Addressing the Thorny Issues

I n this section I look at some issues I think are important. I try to give my reasons for such and what my approach to them would be. If these ideas generate a good conversation, I will be pleased.

What Rationale?

What is the rationale for reforming schools via large-scale assessments? This seems like a good question, somehow. If the assessments are to be worthwhile and useful, they will be attending to certain purposes and functions for particular reasons; that is, they have a rationale to sustain them.

An Economic Rationale

A Nation at Risk (National Commission on Excellence in Education, 1983), a document said to be the catalyst for the recent wave of educational reform in the United States, sounded an ominous warning. It suggested that the United States was fundamentally threatened by the strength of the economies of other nations and that if our schools did not do a better job of preparing students for the workforce, life as we knew it would be forever gone. Of its five major recommendations, the following three are directly related to assessment: content, standards, and expectations. Although *A Nation at Risk* (National Commission on Excellence in Education, 1983) had its critics, its economic rationale fueled the resulting school reform efforts. World-class standards were needed in schools to bolster the U.S. economy. The spate of assessment activities that followed were based on the premises of that booklet and put assessment activities at the top of the heap of hopes for pushing (or pulling) educational reform.

Berliner and Biddle (1995), citing statistics from sources similar to those used in *A Nation at Risk* (National Commission on Excellence in Education,

1983) to invent an economic rationale for school reform, provided an opposite view. They reinterpreted those same results (and, in places, found that *A Nation at Risk* made assertions without evidence) deciding that U.S. schools were doing reasonably well, thank you. This was despite the fact that overall investments in education in the United States did not meet the levels of other industrialized nations. There was, according to those writers, no crisis. Instead, there was serious school bashing by the Reagan and Bush administrations. They were concerned that otherwise astute policy makers had been taken in.

The Thomas B. Fordham Foundation (1998) 25 years later found the nation still at risk. (I must admit this came from an unlikely source because their perspective on things is so very different from mine.) Interestingly enough, they decided that the United States did not face danger of economic decline, but still the schools needed to be reformed.

It is no wonder the Fordham Foundation had to question the economic rationale. As I write this, the United States is in its longest period of sustained economic growth since World War II. The stock market is booming. The rate of inflation is low. Unemployment is at historically low levels. The U.S. economy is the envy of the developed world.

Pundits say the economic success is a result of increased productivity by American workers. They go on to say that the increased productivity is a function of technology. Where did the labor force learn the technology or the more basic skills (such as reading, writing, and arithmetic) that it needs to master it? No one gives credit to the training that persons receive at school, but certainly schools have played a part in developing characteristics of students that allows them to be adaptable, flexible, and productive as workers. Where are the kudos for schools?

To be honest, I never really thought an economic rationale was a very compelling one. The relationships between education and the economy are complex. The rationale is too simplistic. There is no one-way street where good schools lead to strong economies, as the rationale suggests. Perhaps strong economies produce good schools!

Other Rationales

There are, as they say, books written about other ways to view the aims of schooling in the United States. The economic rationale is but one of a number of rationales. Each of the others, or some combination, could form a basis for wanting to reform or improve schools or assess the outcomes of schooling.

A Talent Rationale

There is a kind of individualistic rationale. Schools should be places where students can pursue their intellectual interests and develop their talents. Students come to schools different in many ways. Those differences should be recognized, responded to, and refined. A good school system is one where students can develop their talents and pursue their interests.

A Social Mobility Rationale

Closely linked with the above is the notion that schools, through the development of diverse talents, can provide opportunities for students to improve their lot. Students can create for themselves a better life than that of their parents by successfully navigating the demands of the school. Schools should be vehicles to escape poverty, low social status, and other social constraints. Upward social mobility through education is a persistent theme of those who hope for the best from our public schools.

A Good Citizen Rationale

Citizenship, another rationale for better schools, is an enduring theme in American educational thought. Schools should promote democratic values and encourage participation in democratic processes. Experiences in schools should not only provide academic skills but also attitudes and perceptions that are consistent with a democratic way of life. Schools should operate to produce good citizens. Good citizens are literate, numerate, and open-minded participants in a democratic way of life.

Rationales and Assessments

I gave a brief sketch of the rationales to make an obvious point: A particular rationale might lead to a distinctive kind of assessment. *A Nation Still at Risk* (Thomas B. Fordham Foundation, 1998) says,

> A dual system, separate and unequal, is being created, almost 50 years after it was declared unconstitutional. Equal educational opportunity is the next great civil rights issue. By this is meant the true equality that comes from providing every child with a first-rate elementary and secondary education. The main renewal strategies should be the implementation of standards, assessments, accountability, and the acceptance of pluralism, competition, and choice.

If the next great issue were equal opportunity, what would the standards and assessments look like? One obvious difference would be a need to emphasize OTL standards, but what other changes would be necessary?

I indicated earlier that one of the first things that happened to the Kentucky assessment was that it eliminated some of the goals that were to be assessed. The two that did not survive were self-sufficiency and effective group membership. It is interesting to me that those are most closely linked with a good citizen rationale. It is also interesting that in a statewide survey when citizens were asked to respond to a variety of issues about the Kentucky reform, those two were the goals most highly regarded by the citizenry (Berger, Hougland, & Kifer, 1993).

To take those goals seriously would, I believe, change the assessment dramatically. For example, no longer could I tell my students that only in schools is cooperation called cheating. That is, working together would become a salient feature of both instruction and assessment.

Learning to work together may provide substantial measurement problems (How does one get at it?). Yet, if it is an important goal and if one is assessing in schools what is important, then it should be assessed.

Self-sufficiency is another outcome not easily measured. My notion would be, however, that if it is there, if it is important, and if one is assessing what is important, an assessment has to have it. An assessment should define ways to gather evidence that shows schools are successfully moving students to more autonomous actions and behavior.

Suppose You Cannot Assess All of the Important Things?

Schools have multiple functions and purposes. It is unreasonable to think that assessments could cover adequately all of the things schools do. I doubt that assessments can cover all of the important things schools do. By their nature, assessments will be of outcomes that are narrower than the range of schooling outcomes. The questions are how much narrower and what are the consequences of the narrowness.

What will be narrowed and what will be assessed depends, I hope, on the rationale for the assessment and its internal coherence. I think an assessment based on a good citizen grounds, however, would look very different from what now exists. It would, for example, look at cognitive outcomes as a means to an end rather than ends in themselves. There would be more intense scrutiny of the narrowing of outcomes through assessing the easiest things to assess. It would emphasize opportunities at least equally with outcomes. It would change the nature of what we thought was important to monitor or evaluate.

Assessments Can Narrow Things in at Least
Four Ways: One of them Is Desirable

I think those who believe that "what you test is what you get" (WYTWYG) are mainly wrong. You get some of what you test, not all of it. You get lots of other outcomes that are not typically assessed.

As Stake (1999) suggested, you also get unintended consequences, although he limited his to the negative. Vitali (1993) showed that elementary school teachers were more likely to adopt innovations in assessment than were middle school or high school teachers. Teachers of younger children in his study were much more likely to change their instruction and attempt to align it with the assessment.

Alignment, too, is problematic. Frameworks and content standards are usually wide in scope. Although they do not contain everything in a curriculum, they are, at best, broad statements of what is desirable. Persons who construct assessments based on the standards enjoy wide latitude in defining questions and the forms of the questions. Different persons with the same framework will come up with sufficiently varied item sets to make the assessment different enough to worry about. Finally, two teachers, equally conscientious, will realistically approach the alignment task differently and are likely to produce distinct changes in their instruction.

Having said all that, I still believe there is a sense in which assessments, especially those with high stakes attached to them, influence profoundly what is taught and learned. There is a piece of truth to WYTWYG.

Fewer Goals

Assessments do narrow things. As in the Kentucky case, they can narrow the set of desirable outcomes. Assessments built on all of Kentucky's learning goals would certainly be different than assessments based on two thirds of them. To measure a subset of goals rather than all of the goals is one way to narrow expectations for students and likely the instruction they receive.

Equally problematic may be that important goals that are difficult to measure may be the first to be eliminated. Allegedly, John Tukey, the inventor of boxplots, said that if something is worth doing, it is worth doing badly. If goals are important and assessments are to linked to the goals, the assessment should contain what is important even if it cannot be easily measured.

Limited Processes

Closely linked to narrowing the goals is narrowing what are considered desirable processes. An assessment to certify students, particularly if it is high stakes, runs the risk of emphasizing the so-called basics, for example, at the expense of equally important advanced outcomes. Students should learn to decode words, spell, and compute. Forget about figuring out the perspective from whence a writer comes, writing a convincing justification of something, or learning to think mathematically. This is the second way, not assessing relevant processes, that assessments narrow things in undesirable ways.

Selected Content

A third way an assessment can corrupt things is through an emphasis on a subset of content areas. Find a large-scale assessment that does not include reading and mathematics. On the other hand, finding assessments that include foreign language, vocational skills, health and physical education, art, or drama is a more difficult task.

I had an experience that convinced me that taking assessments too seriously is even more dangerous than I had imagined. Because I was a member of a districtwide committee, I learned that the school system was to experiment with foreign language learning in three, yet to be chosen, elementary schools. Because I then had a child in elementary school, I went to the principal to see if she was interested in becoming one of the schools. She told me that there was no way the school could do that. In the previous assessment, students had not done well in dictionary skills so they had to emphasize those in the coming year.

An assessment should not determine whether one teaches dictionary skills or foreign languages. I, of course, would teach the foreign language, not the dictionary skills, but that is just me. The important point is that to teach one, both, or none of the areas should be decided on the basis of what students should be experiencing in that school. If a principal can give such a glib answer on the basis of low test scores, here is another area where assessments narrow in exactly the wrong ways.

Depth, not Breadth

Imagine frameworks or content standards notable for their depth, not breadth. Imagine, too, an assessment that sampled well the domains of the framework. What one would have is a situation where an assessment responded positively to the admonitions of those who wrote *A Splintered Vision* (Schmidt et al., 1997) and *Facing the Consequences* (Schmidt et al., 1999). If that assessment narrowed the curriculum so fewer topics were covered in greater depth, it would be narrowing it in a desirable way. It would be a first step toward countering the phenomena of curricula that are a "mile wide and inch deep." It might increase the rigor of the curriculum and produce results that those interested in reform would be pleased with.

Emphasizing depth over breadth involves making tough decisions about what will be assessed in what ways. This is why a rationale for the assessment must be coherent and persuasive. Those who plan assessments must be able to convince others that they have such a rationale. They must also be able to convince others that it is a rationale worth having.

Performance assessments and depth. I have hopes that performance assessments can play a major role in producing assessments of depth, not breadth. I also have hopes they will provide ways to assess connections between content areas and reflect the integration of areas, an additional way to emphasize depth over breadth. There is no doubt in my mind that well-formulated performance events can successfully demand responses from students that can be gotten no other way. Whether they will triumph in the assessment arena is the question (for a less optimistic view, see Haertel, 1999).

Portfolios, performance assessments, and depth. Using portfolios wisely in areas that are to be assessed is one very good way to gather evidence that reflects the depth of understanding a student possesses. Because the work can be collected over time rather than in a one-shot testing session, the assessment can place emphasis on substantive, often long-term tasks that require students to demonstrate their abilities to delve in depth in a subject and also make connections between various content areas.

The art of item writing. The biggest slip twixt cup and lip in assessment work is that of writing items to fit frameworks that often are very broad and ambiguous. Even with well-elaborated frameworks, item writing is idiosyncratic. Figure 5.1 contains the first two NAEP history items reported by Williams et al. (1995). I use them to illustrate the difficulties of creating items that map directly into a framework.

Let us look closely at the items. Are they good questions in the sense that it would be desirable for fourth graders to be able to respond correctly to them? I think the answer is an unambiguous "yes." They are good questions in that sense. Although they require some factual knowledge, they are not bound to a particular set of facts, and they allow the student to respond in thoughtful ways, particularly in the first question where the student is asked to draw inferences from data.

How are they linked to the framework? Notice how much more difficult it is to answer that question. The first question is a historiography question. How do historians know what they know, or what inferences do historians make based on the evidence they see? Notice there is no place in the theme section of the main framework for that kind of item. Also, the item could fit in almost any of the periods. How did the item writer come up with that particular item? Why not get at a similar process by asking students to look at a list of artifacts from a deserted town and ask them, for instance, to name two historical things they learned from the artifacts?

The choice of the item will, of course, influence the difficult, and complexity of the assessment. One hundred idiosyncratic items will produce a test that

---

History Items

Here are examples of two history questions aimed at fourth graders:

I. **You are writing a history report about an old town. What kinds of historical things could you learn about the old town from its cemetery?**

Name two historical things you could learn.

1. _____

2. _____

An **Appropriate** response correctly identifies two historical things one could learn from a cemetery, such as causes of death or family names and relationships.

A **Partial** response correctly identifies one historical thing or it identifies two things, but the second is incorrect. (An example of an unacceptable piece of information is, "what kinds of flowers people liked to put on graves.") Or one or both responses is vague (e.g., "about the people who lived there.")

II. **Your teacher has asked you to teach your classmates about ONE of the following famous places where an important event in American history happened:**

the Alamo
Pearl Harbor
Gettysburg
Roanoke Island

My famous place in history is _____

Write down three facts about the place that you have chosen that will help you teach you classmates about that place.

Fact 1 _____

Fact 2 _____

Fact 3 _____

A **Complete** answer gives three facts that are relevant to the particular place and that would help another person understand the place, such as that the bombing of Pearl Harbor caused the United States to enter WWII, or that the battle of Gettysburg was a turning point in the Civil War.

An **Essential** answer gives two facts that are relevant to the particular place and that would help another person understand the place.

A **Partial** answer gives one fact that is relevant to the particular place and that might help another person understand the place.

Figure 5.1. NAEP History Items
SOURCE: Williams et al. (1995)

Kifer, E., *Large-Scale Assessments: Dimensions, Dilemmas, and Policy.* Copyright © 2001, Corwin Press, Inc.

may or may not sample well the framework. They would certainly sample it differently than would 100 other idiosyncratic items.

Item 2 has interesting properties as well. Notice, for example, that the famous places selected come from different geographic areas and different periods. The item belongs, I believe, in the theme of the changing role of America in the world. Depending on the place a student chooses, the period could be the 1580s, 1720s, 1830s, 1860s, or the 1940s. How did the item writer decide on those places? Why not Plymouth Rock, Eureka, Bull Run, and the Bay of Pigs?

The point of course is not that the question is a bad one. Rather, there are two main points. First is the issue of how idiosyncratic a question can be. Two persons working alone for a week asked to write 40 history questions based on the same framework are unlikely to come up with any items in common.

The second point is even more important. One set of items is likely to be more difficult for students than the other. That point is crucial when one thinks about proficiency standards, a topic I deal with later. It is difficult to know whether one has high standards on an easy test or hard test. Give another test, try to set a comparable standard, get different results.

What About Stakes?

How much an assessment narrows things and in what ways depends, it is often suggested, on the stakes attached to the assessment. High-stakes assessments for students, teachers, or schools logically should have more powerful effects than low-stakes assessments. The more extreme the consequences, the more schools will change. Perhaps not in the desired direction, however.

Payment by Results (Rapple, 1994) was a system in England and Wales where government funding depended on how well a school's students answered questions posed by school inspectors. It lasted more than 30 years with what appear to be unexpected results.

> Payment by results was a narrow, restrictive, Philistine system of educational accountability that impeded for the second half of the nineteenth century any hope that England's elementary education might swiftly advance from its generally appalling condition during the first half of the century when the theories and practices scorned in the likes of Dickens's *Hard Times* were more the norm than the exception. (Rapple, 1994, p. 4)

Assessments such as NAEP or TIMSS may or may not change things as much or as quickly because they are not directly linked to day-to-day activities in the school and are, arguably, low-stakes assessments, or so the thinking would go. Such assessments must rely on the visibility of their results and the power of their interpretations to produce changes. Hence, they are not as effective as agents of change as are assessments that have, say, rewards and sanctions. High-stakes assessments capture the attention of their targets in more immediate and consequential ways. No wonder so many persons believe in high-stakes assessments.

I question these assumptions about high stakes. Furthermore, I believe there are enough unintended consequences of high-stakes assessments to make them suspect.

Think of the accoutrements of today's large-scale assessments. We have adopted frameworks, content standards, proficiency standards, and the like to promote higher academic achievement. Their wholesale adoption has not come from intimidation. Instead, persons who thought they had a better mousetrap convinced others to buy it. NCTM standards may be adopted or not, but the user decides. Despite the hostility to and controversies surrounding proficiency standards when NAEP first introduced them, they now are the coin of the realm. I doubt that the results of any educational study have been more publicized than those of TIMSS. In the public conversation, the insights of *Facing the Consequences* (Schmidt et al., 1999) will either be acted on or not. Performance assessments were not forced on people; they entered the assessment arena through the power of persuasion and dissatisfaction with existing measurement approaches. New and better kinds of assessments were tied to reform efforts because one set of persons, often called policy makers, convinced another set, often called consumers, that such policies and programs were better than what was in place.

That conversion stops when it gets to students, teachers, and schools. The diagnosis is that they cannot be convinced so they have to be coerced. Hence, the need for high stakes and drastic consequences. I do not know why the conversion stops there, and I do not know why the approach to changing instruction and schools does not take the form of working with persons and showing them the better way to do what it is they do. There is no obvious reason why the conversation can operate well at levels of the educational hierarchy above the school, but not work well there. I do know, however, that there is no unimpeachable evidence for the efficacy of high-stakes assessments. In fact, most of the research work with which I am familiar finds such accountability models suspect (see, e.g., Koretz, 1996; Koretz, Barron, Mitchell, & Stecher, 1996; Koretz, Mitchell, Barron, & Keith, 1996).

The major criticisms of high-stakes accountability models are tied to their unintended negative consequences. In Kentucky, high stakes drove out exemplary assessment and returned what was previously considered inferior assessment techniques. They narrowed the curriculum in unintended and negative ways. They created an atmosphere where teacher morale declined. A colleague recently told me that he was in a school that eliminated recess so kids could work on practice examinations. Others have told me about children who are placed in what they call "portfolio prison" because they have not completed all of their portfolio assignments.

The score for a high-stakes accountability system is high on focusing people's attention. If that were the only outcome, it would be difficult to argue against them. The huge unintended negative consequences of such systems are what make me want to eliminate such practices.

High stakes are attached to assessments by those least closely involved with day-to-day activities of the schools. This top-down approach to assessment and school reform goes counter to what one knows about how innovation works best. Let the stakes, high or low, emerge from the experiences and views of those closest to schools and schooling.

A Short Note on Accountability

Accountability systems that rely mainly or exclusively on student test scores should be required to use a small *a*. When such systems use a capital *A*, otherwise thoughtful people forget the myriad forms of accountability that teachers, schools, and school systems actually face. Ask our local superintendent who lost 2 million dollars of state funds for alleged mismanagement of special education programs about accountability. Or ask our mayor, who when she visited the high school with the largest proportion of minorities in the city to find out what she might to do foster positive race relations, was told by the students they could take care of that. How about fixing our roof and giving us useable textbooks! Or, ask teachers about accountability. They respond daily to both reasonable and unreasonable requests from parents, administrators, and the public.

The Need for an External Criterion

I can make statements about the lack of evidence showing that high-stakes testing produces unambiguous positive results because it is difficult to know to what one should compare state assessment results. Such comparisons are difficult, if not impossible, because each state assessment is based on a different framework, defines different standards, and uses different tests. Scores on state assessments inevitably show progress over time. The big question is whether those score increases represent more knowledge or just more familiarity with the test or the assessment.

Again, I use Kentucky as an example. Many schools have increased their accountability indexes appreciably and have received monetary rewards for their efforts. Yet, scores on other tests (ACT, SAT, state-by state NAEP) taken by Kentucky students do not show the same increasing trend. Koretz, Barron, et al. (1996) did a thorough investigation of the apparent discrepancy between large increases in the Kentucky assessment scores and small changes in these other external measures. They concluded that much of the change in Kentucky's assessment was simply scores being inflated by students gaining more familiarity with the test rather than real growth. Their careful study, however, acknowledges the difficulty of finding a defensible external criterion for establishing the validity of a state assessment.

I personally believe that because the tests—NAEP, SAT, ACT—are so different and the frameworks on which they are based so varied, that one should not expect parallel results. I hope my explication of those things in this book is convincing on that matter. In general, however, that argument seems not to win the day.

The second kind of insight I would provide does not gather much support, either. I believe the best way to convince the public that improved scores are reflections of important gains is to give lots of examples of the results of an assessment. One of the problems of state assessments is that they produce and disseminate mainly abstract, complex summary scores. In Kentucky, the accountability index is a weighted sum of several tests scores plus additional variables such as attendance and drop-out rates. With such a highly aggregated score, it is difficult to know whether, for instance, students are getting better in, say, mathematics.

I think it is important to give concrete examples of assessment results rather than reporting mainly an abstract, highly aggregated sum. If the assessment is a good one, examples of portfolio work, responses to good questions, performances on assessment tasks, good essays on writing tasks, and other concrete evidence of student works carefully, but honestly, depicted should provide good information. From what I can garner, not many states provide such good reporting to their constituents.

There is a difficult problem here in producing information that various audiences need rather than what they want. I believe that the type of information listed above is what should be provided to the various audiences for assessment results. Often, however, an audience wants something such as a ranking or normative information. The key is to find a way to substitute the good information for that which is limited. Providing rankings (see the section of school comparisons below) and normative information, for example, are easily digested but superficial (and often misleading), information about performance. They are easy ways out of the harder problem of providing defensible descriptions of outcomes.

Ways to Think About Finding an External Criterion

The public seems to want additional evidence that score increases mean fundamental improvement. Hence, the need for an external criterion or a way to validate the gains. For example, if a state could embed a sizeable portion of its assessment in state-by-state NAEP and have a sizeable portion of NAEP's assessment embed in its, it would be provide an opportunity to make some important comparisons.

I use this example because it would provide a particular state with comparisons with all other states in the NAEP assessment. The model, however, could be applied to fewer entities. That is, states could form coalitions that would enable them to validate their achievement gains. At least the public would have comparative data for something greater than their particular state.

If states had defensible external criteria, then both districts and schools would be able to express their results in terms of outside entities. Such a validation, one hopes, would increase the perceived legitimacy of the assessment and its results.

Level Playing Fields

When a large-scale assessment compares students or schools, there is an assumption made that the comparisons are fair ones—one is comparing apples to apples and oranges to oranges. In both cases, there is a body of evidence that suggests that comparisons may not be fair. Surely one of the first axioms of a good assessment is that there should be a level playing field for all participants.

What exactly is a level playing field? That is not an easy question by any means. I think, however, that defensible score comparisons can be made when there are common opportunities, comparable resources, and learning occurs in similar contexts. I address these issues below.

Student-Level Score Comparisons

Score comparisons between students inevitably raise issues about fairness to poor and minority students. We assume that comparisons are made between persons with similar experiences within our schools. The evidence suggests, however, that poor and minority students do not get comparable experiences to wealthier and majority students.

The most obvious example has to do with curricular differences. Students from homes of lower social status have different curricular experiences within schools. Fewer take advanced courses in secondary school and therefore tend to have lower scores than their wealthier peers. Those score comparisons, therefore, are not so much between students as between the experiences they have. I mentioned earlier the *Debra P. v. Turlington* (1981) case that argued that students who failed a Florida proficiency examination did so because they were not given the opportunity to learn the material on the test. As I write this, several states are weathering lawsuits that suggest that students are not getting the essential opportunities to learn what they should learn to pass certification assessments. It is likely that most such assessment programs will get intense scrutiny and be faced with litigation.

I believe that it is morally right to insist on fair comparisons. That is why I think it is necessary to have both equal opportunities for students and extra unequal opportunities for those who seem to have fallen behind. Each student should have the opportunity to experience the best of what a school offers.

States that have high stakes, minimal competence examinations, or high school leaving examinations are particularly vulnerable to charges by minorities and the poor of unequal access to opportunities that are related to acceptable performance on the test. I believe that the charges are true and should be responded to. That is part of the reason for insisting on coherence across the assessment grid.

I will suggest later that there are desirable reforms that could level the playing field. Right now I would insist that the least that should be done is to provide additional support for students who may not get the opportunities they deserve.

Comparisons Between Schools

If score comparisons are made between schools, another but somewhat similar set of fairness issues arises. It is a fact that on the average, schools with large proportions of poor and minority students score lower than schools with similarly small proportions. Is it fair to compare a school with a large proportion of students from low-income families with one with a large proportion of students from high-income families?

A colleague and I (Guskey & Kifer, 1990, 1999) looked at Kentucky data twice, almost a decade ago and more recently, to determine the relationships among and between some of these variables. In 1990, when schools were being ranked on their average performance, we found that adjusting the scores by the percentage of minority students and those on free and reduced lunches altered dramatically the rankings. Schools with high initial rankings fell because their performance was not so high as expected given their small proportions of poor and minority students. Conversely, low-scoring schools tended to go up in the rankings because they were doing better than expected given their high proportions of poor and minority students.

Findings of relationships between the composition of the student body and test scores is a consistent one and not unique to Kentucky. Virtually every study that I know of finds these same kinds of results. It is easier to teach and learn in some schools than it is in others.

Fairness says that such relationships should not be ignored.

Different Relationships for
Different Types of Outcomes

However one defines outcomes, be they status or change, there are negative relationships between the percentage of students on free or reduced lunch, a common proxy for poverty, and those outcomes. Our second study was with more recent data. We were interested in knowing the effects of these background variables on measures of both status and change. Figure 5.2 shows these relationships for four outcome variables.

Figure 5.2 shows relationships among three predictor variables that include the 1996 Accountability Index (96Index), percentage of students on free or reduced lunch (PFreRed), percentage of students who are minorities (Mpercent), and four outcome variables that include the 1998 Accountability Index (98Index), the difference between 1998 and 1996 (Raw Gain), differences between 1998 and 1996 based on a statistical adjustment (ResGain), and the percentage of improvement from 1996 to 1998 (PerImp). The highest correlation, .7, among the variables is between the two indexes. Schools with high scores in 1996 tend also to have high scores in 1998. The values relevant to this discussion are those in the middle column—the relationships between free and reduced lunch and the four outcomes. Notice that in each case they are negative (and in each case statistically significant). Schools with larger proportions of poor children do worse regardless of the outcome measure.

The largest negative correlation is between PFreRed and the status measure, 1998 Index. The other values are lower, with the lowest being between PFreRed and Percent Improvement. No matter which outcome variable, the background characteristics of students are related to the outcome.

These relationships make the Kentucky Accountability Index suspect on fairness grounds. Figure 5.3 shows how Kentucky defined progress over time and set targets for improvements. Notice that School A has 20 years to reach the goals, whereas School B has only 6 years. It is more likely that a low-scoring school will contain larger proportions of poor and minority students. Yet, despite this, they are expected to improve more rapidly than the high-scoring school.

I do not believe that fair comparisons between schools can be made without some form of adjustment to compensate for the composition of the student body. In the example above, lower-scoring schools are expected to make more rapid improvement because they are given the same amount of time to reach the particular and arbitrary goal of 100. A more equitable way to approach the problem would be to give lower-scoring schools additional time to reach the standard. Fixing both the standard and time creates the inequity. If one wants to hold constant the standard, then fairness would say that the amount of time allowed to reach the standard should vary.

Other kinds of things can be done to make fairer comparisons. The first is to compare a school's performance with that of other schools with similar

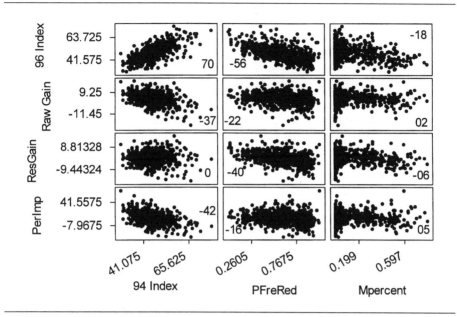

Figure 5.2. Relationships Between Status and Growth Outcomes and Background Characteristics

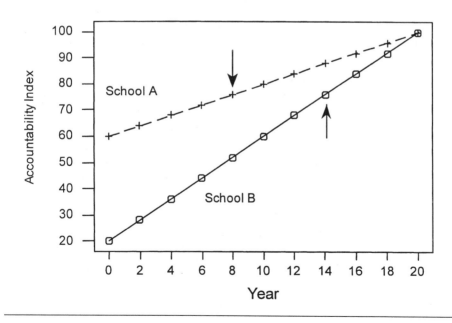

Figure 5.3. Kentucky's Accountability for Two Imaginary Schools

demographic characteristics. That is, create groups or strata of schools with similar student body compositions and then make the comparisons. For one example, California has done this.

A second approach to the problem is to make a more rigorous statistical adjustment. The Tennessee Value-Added Assessment (Sanders, 1998) adjusts for differences within schools before making between-school comparisons. This model is statistically complicated but addresses the problems of making fairer comparisons. Regardless of the model, fairness dictates an adjustment.

The Problem of Standards

It is difficult to argue against standards. It is even more difficult to argue against high standards. Both appear to have captured the public imagination. It is not difficult, however, to worry about what scores mean in the context of standards, be they high or otherwise, and it is easy to worry about whether standards-based improvement goals, targets for increased test scores over time, are realistic.

Musick (1998) compared student performance on the state-by-state NAEP assessment with student performance on their respective states' assessment. For example, he compared the percentage of students who were proficient or higher according to the NAEP assessment with the percentage who were proficient or higher in their state. He found that students, in general, fared better on their own assessment than on NAEP's. That is, they were more likely to be labeled proficient on the state assessment.

Musick's (1998) interpretation of that general finding was that states had not set sufficiently high standards. Such an interpretation might have legitimacy if each of the assessments had similar structures. Careful scrutiny of the dimensions and factors of the assessment grid indicates that is not the case.

State assessments have different purposes and functions. They have different frameworks, content standards, proficiency standards, and test types. The content standards are most likely not only different but vary widely; the proficiency standards serve different purposes—certifying rather that comparing, for example. In short, state assessments vary across virtually all dimensions of the assessment grid. They are more unique than similar.

NAEP state-by-state assessments are particular as well. They are not and are not meant to be similar to individual state assessments. Direct and valid comparisons between NAEP results and results of statewide assessments, therefore, are difficult to make. To choose one dimension to compare as Musick did is to miss the amazing diversity among the assessments. More realistically, he should have said that such comparisons are extremely difficult to make.

I live in a world where one often compares apples and oranges. I think there are legitimate comparisons to be made among them. If I might be facetious, however, Musick's comparisons are a fruit basket. I cannot understand how he chose one dimension on which to compare those different fruits. A proper interpretation begins, I believe, with the recognition that these assessments are different. Because they are so different, it is unreasonable to compare them solely on the basis of achievement levels.

Linn and Baker (1999), in a more defensible way, compared improvement goals for three states: Colorado, Connecticut, and Louisiana. They were the states that gained most in the NAEP state-by-state reading assessments between 1994 and 1998. Using two sets of improvement criteria (Colorado's rules for school accreditation and Kentucky's accountability system), they asked the question of whether these three large growth states would meet the goals defined for them by the Kentucky or Colorado standards.

Colorado has the following two rules: The percentage of fourth graders in a school scoring at or above the proficient level is expected to increase 25% in 3 years, and their third-grade classes are to reduce the percentage of students scoring below grade level by 25% within 3 years. Remember that Kentucky's rules are to subtract a school score from 100 and give schools 10 equal 2-year intervals to reach that target.

To make a long story short, Linn and Baker (1999) found that, despite the fact that Colorado, Connecticut, and Louisiana made the most progress of any in the NAEP assessments, their scores did not increase enough to meet any of Kentucky's or Colorado's targets.

There are troubling issues embedded in this example. The big one is the question of how the targets are set. What was the research or evidence that led to deciding that there should be an x percent increase in y years? I do not believe that such evidence exists. Each state has its own way to use assessments to influence school improvement. Those assessments are idiosyncratic. Standards, as I indicated earlier, are judgments and guesses. They are arbitrary. So, one has idiosyncratic assessments and arbitrary standards to use for growth targets.

The units on which the growth targets are based are problematic as well. Improving 1/10 of the way to 100 every 2 years on an accountability index implies one scale for change. Increasing the percentage at or above a proficiency level is another. Reducing the percentage below grade level is a third. Linn and Baker's (1999) work suggests that each target produces different results in interpreting the large changes in NAEP scores for Colorado, Connecticut, and Louisiana.

The targets offered by Colorado and Kentucky are a combination of wishful thinking and arithmetic. It is not clear on what basis the targets were defined or what was the scale for improvement. Arbitrary proficiency standards may have been turned into capricious growth targets.

A second problem with the existing growth targets or standards is that they are confusing. Kentucky's suffers from its complexity. It is difficult, if not impossible, to tell how changes in a particular component of the accountability index is related to changes in the whole index. Likewise, it is difficult to know how changes across time in the individual components are related to improvement targets.

Colorado's target suffers because it is counter to common sense. To decrease the percentage of students below grade level is to change what it means to be "at or above" grade level. Being at grade level is defined as having a score equal to the mean score in the grade. On the face of it, the Colorado target seeks to have everyone at or above the mean—a statistical impossibility. To be fair to Colorado, they use an average score from a previous test to define the grade level. Thus, it would be possible to have everyone above average. Still, that is confusing, or worse, misleading.

My Arithmetic

I did some arithmetic based on the Kentucky standards for elementary schools. The average accountability score was about 48, and the scores had a standard deviation of about 7. In educational research, a big effect is to be able to change something one standard deviation. Thus, one can ask how many standard deviations would it take to move the average elementary school to the Kentucky target value of 100. The answer is about 7—a 7 standard deviation increase would give the average school a score of 97 (48 + [7 mul 7]). The lowest scoring school would have to improve 10 standard units; the highest about 3.5 standard units. Those are incredible changes!

In the accountability period from 1996 to 1998, the average elementary school gained about 3 points on the Kentucky Accountability Scale. With that amount of average gain per year it would take the highest scoring school about 17 years to reach the target. Comparable values for the average school and the lowest scoring school are 35 and 47 years, respectively. We need patience!

I indicated earlier the power of standards-based score interpretations. It takes one out of the normative mode and into making sense of performance in terms of set levels of expected achievement. That, I believe, is quite a good thing to do.

The other good thing to do is to question whether the standards are good. Are they too high or too low? Are they applied to too many or too few areas? What is the empirical evidence that it is possible to change or grow at the rate that is expected?

The Need for Evidence

To answer these and other relevant questions, we need to know a lot more about standards and what they mean. If I told you that it takes 8 cups of ingredients to make a cake, and that I was going to use 2 cups of flour, 2 cups of milk, 2 cups of butter, and 2 cups of cement, you would tell me that I would not end up with a cake. You know that through experience. Even though my arithmetic is correct—2 + 2 + 2 + 2 = 8—what I get by adding the ingredients together is not a cake.

Right now we do not know enough about standards to be able to bake a standards cake. The levels and growth targets are still just arithmetic and should be approached that way.

CHAPTER 6

Monitoring What Matters

At least two things should be evident to the reader by now. I do not like high-stakes assessments, and I do not believe that assessments by themselves can produce desirable changes in schooling. What I have not said is what I prefer.

I prefer assessments that monitor achievement. They should be used to monitor innovative practices and promising initiatives. The results of the assessments are then used to provide information to students, parents, and schools. The information is such that teachers will use it for the purposes of improving what they are doing.

I believe that there are some initiatives that would produce desirable changes in schools and would be reflected in an assessment that monitored closely what was changed.

Modest Reforms for Large Gains or Big Reforms for Modest Gains

So far, I have talked about the need for coherence across the dimensions of the assessment grid, but I have not said much about systemic reform. Those two notions go hand in hand. Smith, O'Day, and Fuhrman (1992) spoke early about the need for what they called systemic reform. Among its desirable features was a unifying vision, guidelines for curriculum frameworks, professional development, and assessment. These were to be coherent, whole, and systemic. Their alignment would lead to reenergized schools and rapid improvement.

To get the systemic change would not be easy. Fuhrman (1993) elaborated on the political difficulties of obtaining such coherence, again in the context of school reform and improvement. Schools are complex institutions that must respond to multiple constituents with competing agendas. For example, the business community has very different views of schooling than do parents and students. What legislators may want for schools has to be filtered through diverse views that exist among their constituents. Organizing the political wherewithal to produce a consensus of what should be done in schools is by no means an easy task.

I agree with the diagnosis of the difficulties of producing systematic reform. I also agree with the notion that such changes are likely to produce gains in achievement outcomes—the kinds of things that are typically assessed. I disagree that those gains are likely to be large. They will be small at best.

I try to imagine, from a student's point of view, how an aligned, coherent system creates different experiences in school than the ones I had last year.

I will still, in all likelihood, be in the same school with the same facilities, students, and teachers. I will probably be using the same textbooks, required to do the same amount of homework, and be involved in the same extracurricular activities. My friends probably will have not changed. My parents and, more important in the later school years, my peers will have the same views about educational matters. My teachers may tell me that I have to do well on a test and perhaps I will be given some practice in doing so. Perhaps my coursework will be more focused and there will be some external pressure applied for me to do better. I will listen to the same music, watch the same television shows, and hang out in the same places. The things I care about, however, within and without the school will not change much.

Eisner (1990), speaking about reform efforts, expresses the above more eloquently than I in the following: "As noteworthy as these efforts to improve schooling in America have been, they are, alas, but minor themes within the larger score that is American education; more factors are at work to stabilize schools than to change them." Furthermore, "I submit that the 4000-student high school I attended 40 years ago is not fundamentally different, structurally and organizationally, from the high schools operating today" (Eisner, 1990, p. 523).

Even if the hopes of the systemic reformers were to become reality, my guess is that the effects that systemic reform produces on schools are likely to be small, if any. Presently, there is no evidence that suggests much in the way of effects. I understand that systemic reformers would reply that it has not yet happened. Proper alignment has not occurred, but clearly the promises of large achievement gains with what I believe are modest reforms have not yet become evident.

I call the systemic change rationale one that expects modest changes in the structure of schooling to produce major changes in the outcomes of schooling. I propose another, I think more realistic, view. It will take major changes in schooling to produce modest changes in outcomes.

Big Reforms for Modest Gains

Class Size

I have some ideas about what these major changes should be. The first is that there should be very small classes in the early years of a child's schooling.

One of education's enduring research questions is whether small class sizes are better than large class sizes, and, better for what?

Glass (1982) reported his findings of a meta-analysis (a way to do a quantitative synthesis of research findings) of class size research. He found that class sizes below 20 were superior in a variety of ways to those with more than 20. Furthermore, as the size of classes decreased from 20 they became more and more superior.

Despite what appeared to be unequivocal evidence supporting small classes, there remained those who either suspected the research, suspected the conclusions, or both. The class size research seemed not to catch on.

Recently, however, new, persuasive evidence for the efficacy of small classes has emerge from the Student Teacher Achievement Ratio Study (STARS) project, a Tennessee initiative that studied the effects of small classes from 1984 through 1989.

STARS (Finn, 1998; Finn & Achilles, 1990; Mosteller, 1995) is unique in educational research. It is a large-scale, true experiment. Students in kindergarten through the third grade were randomly assigned to one of the following three treatments: (a) small classes of 13 to 17 students, (b) regular classes of 22 to 25 students, and (c) regular classes with both a teacher and a teacher's aide. There were about 100 classes in each of the treatments. Schools in the experiment were stratified to include those in the inner city and rural, urban, and suburban areas.

Results showed higher achievement on standardized tests in reading, language, mathematics, and social studies for students in small classes. Small classes beat both the "regular" classes and the classes with an aide, suggesting that it is not the ratio of adults to children that matters. Rather, it is the number of students in the classroom that counts.

The effects of small classes were larger for minority than majority students (Achilles, 1998; Achilles et al., 1998). That is, the gap between average minority and majority performance was narrowed in small classes. The positive effects of small classes continued through the students' later academic work.

In addition, students who benefited from small class sizes developed a repertoire of other desirable characteristics. They worked harder, took more initiative, and were less likely to be disruptive and inattentive.

Students in the small class size experiment benefited beyond the years of the experiment (Achilles et al., 1996; Nye et al., 1992a, 1992b). The positive effects of their experiences extended at least 2 years after the experiment ended. Getting students off to a good start apparently lasts longer than just the time they spend initially in small classes.

As I write this, the national media is questioning the effects of implementing small class sizes in California. (Actually, the California initiative did not go far enough. It lowered the size to 20 when the research suggested 13-17.) In a nutshell, schools encounter problems securing enough qualified teachers and sufficient numbers of classrooms to accommodate the initiative. Those, of course, are valid concerns. However, they deal with the problems of implementing the change, not the effectiveness of such changes if they were implemented properly.

Rome, they say, was not built in a day. Huge physical changes in schools such as adding twice as many classrooms for kindergarten through third grade cannot occur overnight either. Patience and planning is called for.

Effectively eliminating large classes and substituting small ones changes what students experience during their early schooling. How they experience school is altered. For the first 4 years, pupils are dealing with a smaller crowd. They get more attention and are known better by adults in the school. It makes sense that those 4 crucial years would enhance the students' performance and encourage them to be more responsible school citizens.

Instituting small classes in schools, especially primary schools, is a large, costly change. The change is large enough to influence how a child experiences a school. The results of such changes, what I consider big structural changes, are likely to be modest but important. The effects would likely extend beyond the outcomes now typically assessed and would include more positive attitudes and a healthier participation in school life.

Increasing Participation

Why I Believe Participation Is as Important as Outcomes

Means, statistical averages, are strange beasts. They tell you about centers of distributions but nothing else. Let me give a concrete example.

For decades now, IEA has been interested in the yield of a country's educational system. To put the issue not very precisely, how much knowledge in a particular content area do schools produce? Let us take an international comparison at the end of secondary school for our example.

Suppose in that last year one system has only 50% left of its cohort (students who started together in the first grade), whereas another has 75%. Suppose you give the students in those systems a test and find that the averages are equal. System 1, say, has a mean of 45 and System 2 has a mean of 45. Which system has the greatest yield? In all likelihood, the answer is System 2.

The average for System 2 is based on a higher proportion of the students who remain in school. The yield is greater even though the means do not reveal that important difference.

Figure 6.1 shows issues surrounding participation in mathematics during the terminal year of secondary school in SIMS. The issues here are very different from those of eighth grade. Virtually all students take some type of mathematics in the younger population. By the end of secondary school, depending on the system, a large proportion of the cohort is either no longer enrolled in school or not taking mathematics or both.

The estimated percentage of the cohort still in school ranges from a high value of more than 90% in Japan to lows of 17% in New Zealand and England. The percentage taking advanced mathematics courses ranges from a high of 50% in Hungary to lows of 6% in Israel and New Zealand.

The Hungarian Example

Although most systems are very selective at this level, Hungary is a striking exception. Although only 50% of the cohort are still in school, all of them take advanced mathematics. This system apparently is telling students that advanced mathematical knowledge is so important that every student still in school must have it.

Miller and Linn (1985) examined achievement patterns in light of different retention rates and report two things that are relevant. First, although the average level of achievement for Hungary's students is close to the bottom among the systems, it is very close to the U.S. mean. Second, the top 1% and 5% of Hungarian students perform near the top of the distribution of scores for the systems in the study. From a participation perspective, the Hungarians have it both ways. Not only do they provide advanced mathematical experiences to a large percentage of the cohort and thereby increase dramatically the sum of mathematical knowledge in the culture, but they also do it without sacrificing the talents of their most capable students. As a model for both providing opportunity and creating a pool of talent, Hungary's bears scrutiny.

The U.S. Case

Because the U.S. case is practically the opposite of the Hungarian example, it again deserves scrutiny. The United States has a high retention rate and an average percentage of students taking advanced mathematics. The latter count, however, is misleading. Most of the students who take mathematics at this level are not taking the most advanced mathematics in the schools. Advanced placement calculus is the highest level of mathematics available in U.S. high schools. The participation in that course was about 3% of the cohort. Can you imagine what the yield of mathematics would be if we adopted the Hungarian practice for all of our secondary students?

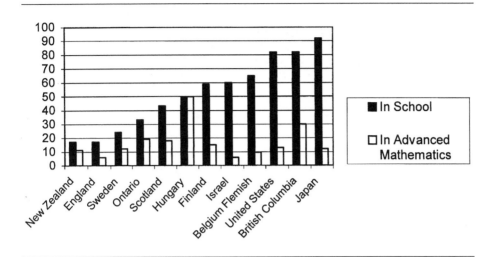

Figure 6.1. Participation Rates in Various International Educational Systems

Differentiated Curriculum and Participation

We could not replicate the Hungarian practice because we would not have many students eligible for advanced placement calculus. We differentiate our mathematics curriculum too early in a student's career for that to occur. To me, *participation* means participation in the best that a school has to offer, but we have policies and procedures that preclude such participation for a majority of our students.

Analyses from SIMS produced a substantial number of results addressing the effects of a differentiated curriculum in eighth grade (Burstein, 1994). Those results are now being replicated in TIMSS and are reported in *Facing the Consequences* (Schmidt et al., 1999).

A pretest was administered in eight educational systems at the beginning of the school year, making it possible to describe how students were allocated to classrooms or schools within those systems. Figure 6.2 depicts these allocations.

In one paper (Kifer, 1984), I described how the variance decomposition (describing whether the variation in scores reflects individual differences, classroom differences, or school differences) reflects decisions made to track students either into homogeneous classrooms or different types of schools. In Figure 6.2, areas of the circles are roughly proportional to the total variation in achievement for each system. The wedges within the circles represent percentages of total variation found between students, classrooms, and schools. The circles containing only two wedges depict systems that did not sample two classrooms per school. In those cases, the variation is labeled student and

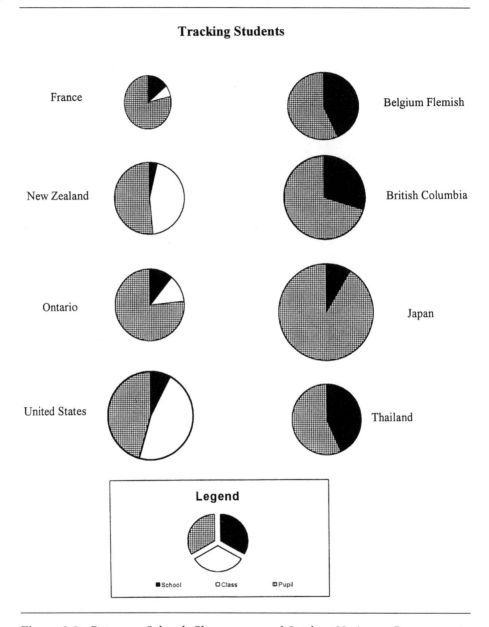

Figure 6.2. Between-School, Classroom, and Student Variance Components for Eight International Systems

school variation although, theoretically, the wedge for school contains both the classroom and school variance. That is, the between-classroom variation, if any exists, is part of the between-school variation, not between-student variation.

The differences between systems are dramatic. Not only are the total variances (individual differences within a system) of strikingly different magnitudes but also that variation (how the system responds to individual differences) is divided in distinct ways. In Japan, for instance, almost all of the large total variation is between students. Because such a small amount of between-school variation exists, variation between classes in the same school must likewise be small. Apparently, the Japanese either ignore individual differences when assigning students to classrooms, or their educational policies produce equality among classrooms and schools. Neither homogeneous grouping in mathematics nor sorting by school takes place in Japan in grade 8.

The United States provides the most extreme contrast to the Japanese pattern of variation. The magnitude of the between-classroom component, which represents tracking in U.S. schools, is its single largest component and exceeds comparable values in all of the other systems.

Although the distinctive patterns of other systems have been discussed elsewhere, the major conclusion is worth repeating. These eight systems demonstrate a variety of practices in sorting, or not sorting, students into different types of classrooms or schools. They range from what is done in Japan, France, and Ontario (where no sorting has yet occurred by grade 8) to what is done in the United States, where more variation in achievement is allocated to sorting practices than to individual differences.

Consequences in the United States

Because the United States shows the largest effect due to tracking, it is worth reporting what is known about the consequences of the policies that produce it. A typical pattern was to form, in any school with a sufficiently large enrollment, the following four types of mathematics classrooms: algebra, pre-algebra, general, and remedial. The typical rationale for this is that homogeneous grouping provides better instruction. What is ignored is that the practice also produces fundamentally different patterns of opportunity, participation, and exposure. In grade 8 in the United States, some students are exposed to mathematics content and experiences that others may never get. This is opposed to what happens in educational systems of countries with no comparable tracking.

Figure 3.3 showed boxplots of OTL ratings by classroom type. It is evident from the figure that tracking students and differentiating the curriculum are two sides of the same coin. Students in algebra classes are exposed to very different kinds of material from those in other classes. Students in remedial classes are exposed to very little mathematics in comparison with other groups and are likely to have been tracked so that they never will be exposed to the material provided to the algebra students.

These practices deny opportunities for the many to experience what the few get, plus other equally undesirable side effects (Kifer, 1984). These include the following:

1. Sorting was replete with misclassifications. Only about one half of the top 10% of students on the arithmetic pretest were placed in algebra; the others were spread among the remaining class types.

2. Sorting favors white female students from wealthy homes. If placement in high-level classes were strictly meritocratic, more boys, more members of ethnic groups other than white, and more children from poor families would be in those classes.

3. Selection is so rigid and so early that it effectively eliminates the major proportion of the cohort from participating in the most advanced mathematics offered by the school system.

Early Tracking

How early and to what degree systems sort and track students is an issue of major consequences for what a system can produce. If findings about mathematics represent what happens in schools, early tracking of students has a profound effect on chances for many to be exposed to learning experiences offered to a tracked elite. The practice of tracking so early effectively eliminates the possibility for most students to experience what is considered the best a school system has to offer. It also, of course, leads to a lack of fairness when making comparisons based on assessment results.

To eliminate tracking and increase participation are not necessarily costly innovations. They would, however, be difficult ones because a lot of minds need to be changed. We live in a culture that believes success in school is more a matter of ability (hence our tracking) than of hard work, effort, or being exposed to exemplary teaching. We need to change the ability mentality to an effort mentality. This might be more difficult than finding the monetary resources for small class sizes. Common school experiences for students is not a new idea.

> Every subject which is taught at all in a secondary school should be taught in the same way and to the same extent to every pupil as long as he pursues it, no matter what the probable destination of the pupil may be, or at which point his education is to cease. (Eliot, 1894, p. 5)

Small Schools

My final big change to produce modest gains in outcomes is small schools. Years of educational research beginning at least with Barker and Gump (1964) has established the efficacy of small schools in terms of a broad array of outcomes. Recent research (Cotton, 1996a; Meier 1995a, 1995b) confirms these initial findings. Students' attitudes toward schools and school subjects (Fowler, 1995; Howley, 1994, 1996; Rutter, 1988) are more positive in small than large schools, and overwhelmingly so. Students in small schools experience stronger feelings of belonging and affiliation, lower levels of alienation (Gregory, 1992), and better interpersonal relations (Fowler & Walberg, 1991). Students in small schools participate in more activities, attend school more regularly, and drop out in smaller proportions (Cotton, 1996b). Evidence suggests that poor and minority students do relatively better in small schools (Lee & Smith, 1997). Finally, there is ambiguity about whether small schools are more costly than large schools. A study in New York City (Stiefel, Iatarola, Fruchter, & Berne, 1998), for example, found that cost per enrolled student was higher in small schools, but the cost on the basis of number of students who graduated was lower.

I teach a class in which the subject of how educational research is used, or not used, often comes up. I use the example of the efficacy of small schools to demonstrate the lack of influence of such research. The small-schools research has 40 years or so of having established the superiority of small over large schools in their social features and related outcomes. Recently, the research finds superiority in the achievement domain as well, although that superiority was not evident in early research. It is clear now that small schools are superior on almost all dimensions. So, now is the time to begin to think about how to introduce more small schools into the public school arena.

Questions of implementation are crucial here just as they are for small classes. How small a school should be is not an absolute. One community may choose to have elementary schools no larger than 200 students; another community could choose 300 students. The context, setting, community, environment milieu set the limits on how small is small enough.

Without getting into the details of how to implement small schools, I will merely mention that there have been some extremely clever attempts to put them in place. Some have experimented with schools within schools where each school has its own staff (Raywid, 1996). Others have found uses for large-school buildings (senior citizen centers) and then replaced them with small schools. Cost-effective ways of achieving smaller schools are available. It is a matter of our creativity and imagination to put them in place.

I heard recently that Indiana U.S. House member Baron Hill's office is sponsoring an initiative on small schools. A bill to fund that initiative is being prepared. It may or may not be debated and voted on. It would, however, be a desirable way for the federal government to support an educational initiative that promises to make schools better places for students.

I do not doubt that moving from large schools to small schools is an expensive proposition, but the value of small schools may outweigh those costs. It would be a big initiative that should produce modest but important changes in what attributes students possess when they exit the public schools.

A Final Note

I would love to design the assessments that evaluated these big changes. So, to let the reader know what parts of the assessment grid I consider the most important to us, I completed Figure 6.3. It is the grid for my assessments of these innovations.

First, the rationale for the assessment would be communitarian or good citizen. I want schools to be places where students develop responsiblity, learn to be productive, and will be, above all, thoughtful citizens.

Purpose. My assessment would focus mainly on using assessments to improve instruction. Although the results would be in the form of achievement and other measures, the main reason for collecting the data would be to inform teachers about the successes they were or were not having.

Function. My assessments would be used mainly for evaluation purposes. They would be formative in the sense that information from them would be fed back to teachers. They would have a summative part because I would like to know if the innovation worked.

Measures. I would measure perennial reading, writing, mathematics, science, and social science as well as general attitudes.

Targets. My main targets would be teachers and their classrooms. Although measurements would be taken of students, a set of results would be given back to teachers to inform their practices.

Standards. I would have frameworks to describe those outcomes I was measuring. I would have neither content standards nor proficiency standards, although some of the measurements I would use would be based on rubrics that included definitions of various levels of performance. I would have OTL standards and assessment standards.

Stakes. There would be no rewards and sanctions. I hope the stakes would be low!

Outcomes. The outcomes would focus on growth or change. I would like them to be primarily longitudinal, at least over the school year.

Assessments. The assessments would be performance assessments and a heavy emphasis would be placed on assessing via portfolios.

Technology. If you got it, use it.

Support. I would place enormous emphasis on providing support for all those involved.

Assessment Grid			
Purposes/	☐ Achievement	☐ Accountability	☒ Instruction
Functions:	☐ Monitor	☐ Certify	☒ Evaluate ☐ Compare
			☒ *Formative* ☒ *Summative*
Measures:	☒ Content	☒ Other	
	☐ *One* ☐ *More than one*		
Targets:	☐ Student	☒ Class/Teacher	☒ School ☐ District/State/Nation
	☒ Elementary	☒ Middle	☒ Secondary
Standards:	☒ Frameworks	☐ Content	☐ Proficiency ☒ OTL
	☒ Assessment		
Stakes:	☐ High	☐ Moderate	☒ Low
	☐ *Rewards* *Sanctions*		
Outcomes:	☐ Status	☒ Growth/Change	
		☐ *Cohort* ☒ *Longitudinal*	
Assessments:	☐ Traditional	☒ Performance	
	☐ *Multiple Choice* *Norm Referenced*	☐ *Constructed Response* ☒ *Performance Events* *Writing on Demand* ☒ *Portfolio*	
Technology	☒ Calculators	☒ Word Processors	☒ Adaptive Devices ☒ Other
Support:	☒ Students	☒ Teachers	☒ Staff
	☐ *Tutoring* *Summer School* *Other*	☐ *Staff Development*	
Reporting:	☒ Students/Parents	☒ Class/Teacher	☒ School ☒ Public

Figure 6.3. The Assessment Grid for My Assessment

Reporting. The first obligation of reporting is to students and parents. I would report not only the measures but also OTL. I mentioned earlier that I would provide feedback to teachers. Hoping that the innovations worked, I would want to report its success to those remaining audiences.

I would love to do those assessments!

RESOURCE

Informative Web Sites

I spent a good deal of time surfing the Internet while writing this book, and I was amazed by the amount of very good material I found. Below, in no particular order, are some of the sites I found most useful. I include their descriptions of themselves or my comments, or both.

National Center for Research on Evaluation, Standards and Student Testing (CRESST)

CRESST's mission is to develop new methodologies for evaluating educational quality; create new designs for assessing student learning; promote the sound use of assessment data; set the national research agenda for assessment; influence practice; and encourage the use of new information technologies.

Address: http://cresst96.cse.ucla.edu/index.htm

Developing Standards Overview

In addition to the description below, this site contains pointers to each state's assessment or standards Web site.

Good teachers have standards in mind when they set their lessons up, where the idea of a "standard" represents a specific idea of what the teacher expects a student to recall, replicate, manipulate, understand, or demonstrate at some point down the road—and of how the teacher will know how close a student has come to meeting that standard. Standards, in other words, are conceptually nothing new—but they did receive a new emphasis over the last decade, through various state initiatives and through the passage of the Goals 2000: Educate America Act. The growth of the Internet has given us the chance to index the sources of information about standards in one place and place that information at anyone's electronic fingertips. We have established this page as a repository for as much information about educational standards and curriculum frameworks from all sources (national, state, local, and other) as can be found on the Internet.

Address: http://putwest.boces.org/Standards.html

Educational Policy Analysis Archives

This is an electronic journal with pointers to each of its previous published works. It has a responsive search engine that allows the user to access quickly needed papers. It contains the complete text of papers about education broadly construed as well as those related to assessment topics.

Address: http://olam.ed.asu.edu/epaa

National Center for Educational Statistics (NCES; from the acting commissioner)

The NCES is the primary federal agency responsible for the collection, analysis, and reporting of data related to education in the United States. Five principal responsibilities are the focus of NCES activities: make the data collected on education available to the public; provide indicators on the status and trends in education; report on the condition of education to Congress, state policy makers, educational practitioners, the media, and the public; assist states and school districts in improving their statistical systems; and review and report on education in other nations.

To fulfill these tasks, the NCES has created a series of databases on a wide variety of topics at the national, state, and local levels addressing both elementary and secondary education and postsecondary education.

These data collections are unique resources for researchers and policy analysts for discussions at the national, state, and local levels. It is important that the role of education for the life of individuals and groups be understood in order to enhance the quality of life in the United States.

Address: http://nces.ed.gov

National Goals Panel

Eight national education goals have been established for the nation as a framework for education reform. As part of this effort, the National Education Goals Panel (NEGP) was created in 1990 to measure the nation's progress toward reaching these goals. The NEGP Web site offers a variety of resources to help you find out about the goals, our nation's and each state's progress toward them, key issues in the area of education reform, and events and programs. Information relevant to schools, districts, and state departments of education can be found.

Address: http://www.negp.gov

Council of Chief State
School Officers (CCSSO)

The CCSSO is a nationwide, nonprofit organization composed of public officials who lead the departments responsible for elementary and secondary education in the states, the U.S. extrastate jurisdictions, the District of Columbia, and the Department of Defense Education Activity. In representing chief education administrators, CCSSO works on behalf of the state agencies that have primary authority for education in each state.

Address: http://www.ccsso.org

U.S. Department of Education

As one might imagine, this site contains an extraordinarily broad array of educational materials and information. The site I give is one way to access quickly information relevant to assessment issues.

Address: http://www.ed.gov/Programs/bastmp/SEA.htm

American Educational Research
Association (AERA)

AERA is concerned with improving the educational process by encouraging scholarly inquiry related to education and by promoting the dissemination and practical application of research results.

AERA is the most prominent international professional organization with the primary goal of advancing educational research and its practical application. Its more than 22,000 members are educators; administrators; directors of research, testing, or evaluation in federal, state, and local agencies; counselors; evaluators; graduate students; and behavioral scientists.

The broad range of disciplines represented by the membership includes education, psychology, statistics, sociology, history, economics, philosophy, anthropology, and political science.

Address: http://www.aera.net

The Third International Mathematics and Science Study (TIMSS– International)–Boston College

Find out about the largest international study of student achievement— which countries participated, how student achievement was measured, what contextual information was collected, and how to obtain the results.

Address: http://wwwcsteep.bc.edu/timss

The Third International Mathematics and Science Study (TIMSS–US)–Michigan State

The TIMSS represents the most extensive investigation of mathematics and science education ever conducted. The study is sponsored by the International Association for the Evaluation of Educational Achievement and funded in the United States by the National Science Foundation and the National Center for Education Statistics. Approximately 50 countries have participated in this comparative survey of education focusing on 9-year-old students, 13-year-old students, and students in their last year of secondary schools. For the oldest students, TIMSS analyses considered the following three groups: a cross-section of all students completing their last year of secondary education (i.e., a "literacy" sample), mathematics specialists (i.e., those students studying or having studied calculus), and science specialists (i.e., those students studying or having studied physics).

Address: http://ustimss.msu.edu

International Association for the Evaluationof Educational Achievement (IEA)

For more than three decades, the IEA has carried out international compara-tive studies focusing on educational policies and practices, covering topics such as mathematics and science education, reading literacy, and computers in education. A current project is underway in mathematics and science (TIMSS) and a project in foreign/second language is in preparation.

The IEA has the intention, for instance by means of this clearinghouse, to offer more results and descriptions of (concluded) studies in electronic for-mat to the research community at large. Not only results in the sense of publi-cations but also the data, codebooks, and questionnaires are being made available by the Data Enhancement Project.

Address: http://uttou2.to.utwente.nl

National Assessment Governing Board (NAGB)

Welcome to the National Assessment Governing Board's (NAGB's) web site. The Governing Board is an independent, bipartisan group whose members include governors, state legislators, local and state school officials, educators, business representatives, and members of the general public. Congress cre-ated the 26-member Governing Board in 1988 to set policy for the National As-sessment of Educational Progress (NAEP)—commonly known as the "The Na-tion's Report Card." In November 1997, Congress granted NAGB exclusive authority over development of the proposed Voluntary National Tests (VNT).

Address: http://www.nagb.org

National Assessment of Educational Progress (NAEP)

The nation's report card, the NAEP, is the only nationally representative and continuing assessment of what America's students know and can do in vari-ous subject areas. Since 1969, assessments have been conducted periodically in reading, mathematics, science, writing, history, geography, the arts, and other fields. By making information on student performance—and instruc-tional factors related to that performance—available to policy makers at the national, state, and local levels, NAEP is an integral part of our nation's evaluation of the condition and progress of education.

Address: http://nces.ed.gov/nationsreportcard/site/home.asp

National Science Foundation (NSF)–EHR

The Directorate for Education and Human Resources (EHR) is responsible for the health and continued vitality of the Nation's science, mathematics, engineering, and technology education and for providing leadership in the effort to improve education in these areas. EHR has five major, long-term goals. To help ensure that a high-quality school education in science is available to every child in the United States and that it is sufficient to enable those who are interested to pursue technical careers at all levels as well as to provide a base for understanding by all citizens.

To help ensure that the educational pipelines that carry all students to careers in science, mathematics, and engineering yield numbers of adequately educated individuals who can meet the needs of the U.S. technical workplace. To help ensure that those who select a career in a science or engineering discipline have available the best professional undergraduate and graduate education and that opportunities are available at the college level for interested nonspecialists to broaden their scientific backgrounds.

To encourage the development of a cadre of professionally educated and trained teachers to ensure excellence in school education for every student and learner. To support informal science education programs and to maintain public interest in and awareness of scientific and technological developments.

Address: http://www.nsf.gov/home/ehr/start.htm

National Council for the Teaching of Mathematics (NCTM)

NCTM represents more than 100,000 mathematics teachers. Through our membership and our more than 250 Affiliated Groups located across the United States and Canada, we reach nearly 200,000 mathematics teachers. Our mission is (a) to provide the vision and leadership necessary to improve the learning of mathematics by all students, (b) to promote excellence in the teaching of mathematics by all teachers, and (c) to serve as an advocate for mathematics education.

NCTM has been a leader in improving mathematics education. Our Standards for curriculum, teaching, and assessment have helped to raise the mathematics achievement levels of our nation's students. NCTM is updating these standards to reflect the current mathematical needs of students, our increased knowledge about teaching and learning, and recent advances in technology. Our new document, "Principles and Standards for School Mathematics," will be released in April 2000.

Address: http://www.nctm.org

ERIC Clearinghouse

The ERIC®Clearinghouse on Assessment and Evaluation seeks to provide 1) balanced information concerning educational assessment and 2) resources to encourage responsible test use.

Address: http://ericae.net

FairTest

The National Center for Fair & Open Testing (FairTest) is an advocacy organization working to end the abuses, misuses and flaws of standardized testing and ensure that evaluation of students and workers is fair, open, and educationally sound.

We place special emphasis on eliminating the racial, class, gender, and cultural barriers to equal opportunity posed by standardized tests, and preventing their damage to the quality of education. Based on four *Goals and Principles,* we provide information, technical assistance and advocacy on a broad range of testing concerns, focusing on three areas: *K-12, university admissions,* and *employment tests.*

FairTest publishes a quarterly newsletter, *The Examiner,* plus a full *catalog* of materials on both K-12 and university testing to aid teachers, administrators, students, parents and researchers. See our order form on this Web site! FairTest also has numerous *fact sheets* available to educate you on standardized testing and alternative assessment.

Address: http://www.fairtest.org

Southern Regional Education Board (SREB)

SREB's home page is designed to help state policymakers and educational leaders more easily access the Southern Regional Education Board's information about elementary, secondary and higher education.

SREB stresses the inseparable links between schools and colleges. Our purpose is to help states improve the quality of education, student opportunity and student achievement.

Although we have made progress in the last several decades, we only have narrowed the gap in student achievement between the South and the rest of the nation. We cannot close this gap unless we set our standards at least as high as those elsewhere in America.

Since the 1960s, the South also has made dramatic progress in higher education access and quality. We have come to recognize that our colleges and universities are our No. 1 asset, our best means of ensuring future prosperity.

SREB turns facts and figures into information that state leaders can use to make decisions about how to improve education. I hope that SREB's home page is useful to you.

Address: http://www.sreb.org/Main/AboutSREB/about.html

American Psychological Association —APA Test Standards

Written for the professional and the educated lay person, Standards for Educational and Psychological Testing is a vitally important reference for professional test developers, sponsors, publishers, users, and students in the fields of education and psychology. The Standards provides guidelines on constructed performance tests, questionnaires, and structured behavior samples.

Address: http://www.apa.org/books/standard.html

References

Achilles, C. M. (1998, April). *If not before: At least now.* Paper presented at the Annual Meeting of the American Educational Research Association, San Diego, CA.

Achilles, C. M., et al. (1996, November). *"This," as Paul Harvey was wont to say, "Is the rest of the story."* Paper presented at the annual meeting of the Mid-South Educational Research Association, Tuscaloosa, AL.

Achilles, C. M., Finn, J. D., & Bain, H. P. (1998). Using class size to reduce the equity gap. *Educational Leadership, 55*(4), 40-43.

Alexander, L., & James, H. T. (1987). *The nation's report card: Improving the assessment of student achievement.* Washington, DC: National Academy of Education.

American Psychological Association and National Council on Measurement in Education. (1997). *Standards for educational and psychological testing.* Washington, DC: American Psychological Association.

Americans With Disabilities Act of 1990, Pub. L. No. 101-336, § 2, 104 Stat. 328 (1991).

Anderson, L. W., & Postlethwaite, T. W. (1989). What IEA studies say about teachers and teaching. In A. Purves (Ed.), *International comparisons and educational reform* (pp. 73-86). Alexandria, VA: Association for Supervision and Curriculum Development.

Anderson, L. W., Ryan, D. W., & Shapiro, B. J. (1989). *The IEA classroom environmental study.* Oxford, UK: Pergamon.

Barker, R. G., & Gump, P. V. (1964). *Big school, small school: High school size and student behavior.* Palo Alto, CA: Stanford University Press.

Beaton, A. E. (1996). *IEA's third international mathematics and science study (TIMSS): Mathematics achievement in the middle school years.* Washington, DC: U.S. Department of Education, Office of Educational Research and Improvement.

Beaton, A. E., & Johnson, E. G. (1992). Overview of the scaling methodology used in the national assessment. *Journal of Educational Measurement, 29*(2), 163-175.

Beaton, A. E., & Zwick, R. (1992). Overview of the National Assessment of Educational Progress. *Journal of Educational Statistics, 17*(2), 95-109.

Berger, M. C., Hougland, J. C., & Kifer, E. (1993). *The Kentucky Education Reform Act and the public: A study of attitudes during KERA's first three years.* Lexington, KY: Institute on Education Reform Series.

Berliner, D. C. (1987). Simple views of effective teaching and a simple theory of classroom instruction. In D. C. Berliner & B. V. Rosenshine (Eds.), *Talks to teachers* (pp. 67-81). New York: Random House.

Berliner, D. C., & Biddle, B. J. (1995). *The manufactured crisis: Myths, fraud, and the attack on America's public schools.* Reading, MA: Addison-Wesley.

Binkley, M., & Rust, K. (Eds.). (1994). *Reading literacy in an international perspective: Collected papers from the IEA reading literacy study.* Washington, DC: U.S. Department of Education, Office of Educational Research and Improvement.

Bloom, B. S. (1968). *Learning for mastery: Evaluation comment.* Los Angeles: University of California at Los Angeles, Center for the Study of Evaluation of Instructional Programs.

Boswell, J. (1922). *The life of Samuel Johnson.* New York: Doubleday.

Bourque, M. L., & Hambleton, R. K. (1993). Setting performance standards on the National Assessment of Educational Progress. *Measurement and Evaluation in Counseling and Development, 26*(1), 41-47.

Burstein, L. (Ed.). (1994). *The IEA study of mathematics III: Student growth and classroom process in early secondary school.* New York: Pergamon.

Burstein, L., Koretz, D. M., Linn, R. L., Sugrue, B., Novak, J., Lewis, E., & Baker, E. L. (1993). *The validity of interpretations of the 1992 NAEP achievement levels in mathematics.* Los Angeles: University of California at Los Angeles, Center for Research on Evaluation, Standards, and Student Testing.

Carroll, J. B. (1975). *The teaching of French as a foreign language in eight countries.* New York: John Wiley.

Comber, L. C., & Keeves, J. R. (1973). *Science education in nineteen countries.* New York: John Wiley.

Cotton, K. (1996a). *School size, school climate, and student performance* (Close-up No. 20). Portland, OR: Northwest Regional Educational Laboratory.

Cotton, K. (1996b). *Affective and social benefits of small-scale schooling* (Document No. EDO-RC-96-5). Charleston, WV: ERIC Clearinghouse on Rural Education and Small Schools.

Council on School Performance Standards. (1989). *Preparing Kentucky youth for the next century: What students should know and be able to do and how learning should be assessed.* Bowling Green: Western Kentucky University.

Debra P. v. Turlington, 644 F.2d 397, 6775 (5th Cir., 1981).

Dewey, J. (1916). *Democracy and education: An introduction to the philosophy of education.* New York: Macmillan.

Diegmueller, K. (1994, November 2). Panel unveils standards for history: Release comes amid outcries of imbalance. *Education Week,* pp. 1-10.

Dossey, J. A., Mullis, I.V.S., & Jones, C. O. (1993). *Can students do mathematical problem solving?* (NCES Report No. 23-FR01). Washington, DC: National Center for Education Statistics, U.S. Department of Education, Office of Educational Research and Improvement.

Educational Commission of the States. (1997). *Education accountability systems in 50 states*. Denver, CO: Author.

Eisner, E. (1990). Who decides what schools teach? *Phi Delta Kappan, 71*(7), 523-525.

Eliot, C. (1894). *Report of the Committee of Ten on secondary school studies*. New York: American Book.

Ferrara, S. F., & Thornton, S. J. (1988). Using NAEP for interstate comparisons: The beginnings of a "national achievement test" and "national curriculum." *Educational Evaluation and Policy Analysis, 10*(3), 200-211.

Finn, J. D. (1998) *Class size and students at risk. What is known? What is next? A commissioned paper*. Washington, DC: National Institute on the Education of At-Risk Students.

Finn, J. D., & Achilles, C. M.. (1990). Answers and questions about class size: A statewide experiment. *American Educational Research Journal, 27*(3), 557-577.

Forsyth, R. A. (1991). Do NAEP scales yield valid criterion-referenced interpretations? *Educational Measurement: Issues and Practice, 10*(3), 3-9.

Foshay, A. W., Thorndike, R. I., Hotyat, F., Pidgeon, D. A., & Walker, D. A. (1962). *Educational achievement of thirteen-year-olds*. Hamburg, Germany: UNESCO Institute for Education.

Fowler, W. J., Jr. (1995). School size and student outcomes. In H. J. Walberg (Series Ed.) & B. Levin, W. J. Fowler, Jr., & H. J. Walberg (Vol. Eds.), *Advances in educational productivity: Vol. 5. Organizational influences on educational productivity* (pp. 214-232). Greenwich, CT: JAI.

Fowler, W. J., Jr., & Walberg, H. J. (1991). School size, characteristics, and outcomes. *Educational Evaluation and Policy Analysis, 13*(2), 189-202.

Frederiksen, N., Mislevy, R. J., & Bejar, I. I. (1993). *Test theory for a new generation of tests*. Hillsdale, NJ: Lawrence Erlbaum.

Fuhrman, S. H. (Ed.). (1993). *Designing coherent education policy: Improving the system*. Washington, DC: U.S. Department of Education, Office of Educational Research and Improvement.

Glaser, R., & Linn, R. L. (1992). *Assessing student achievement in the states. The first report of the National Academy of Education Panel on the evaluation of the NAEP trial state assessment: 1990 trial state assessment*. Washington, DC: National Academy of Education.

Glass, G. V (Ed.). (1982). *School class size: Research and policy*. Beverly Hills, CA: Sage.

Gregory, T. (1992). *Small is too big: Achieving a critical anti-mass in the high school*. Minneapolis, MN: Minnesota University, Hubert H. Humphrey Institute of Public Affairs. (ERIC Document Reproduction Service No. ED 361 159)

Guskey, T. R. (Ed.). (1994). *High stakes performance assessment: Perspectives on Kentucky's educational reform*. Thousand Oaks, CA: Corwin.

Guskey, T. R., & Huberman, A. M. (1995). *Professional development in education: New paradigms and practices.* New York: Teachers College Press.

Guskey, T. R., & Kifer, E. (1990). Ranking school districts on the basis of statewide test results: Is it meaningful or misleading? *Educational Measurement: Issues and Practice, 9*(1), 11-16.

Guskey, T. R., & Kifer, E. (1999, April). *Exploring the relationship between student characteristics and school-level performance assessment results.* Paper presented at the annual meeting of the American Educational Research Association, Montreal, Canada.

Haertel, E. H. (1989). *Report of the NAEP technical review panel on the 1986 reading anomaly and accuracy of NAEP trends, and issues raised by state-level comparisons* (Report No. CS 89-499). Washington, DC: U.S. Department of Education.

Haertel, E. H. (1991). Should the National Assessment of Educational Progress be used to compare the states? *Educational Researcher, 20*(3), 17-22.

Haertel, E. H. (1999). Performance assessment and educational reform. *Phi Delta Kappan, 80*(9), 662-668.

Hazlett, J. A. (1973). *A history of the National Assessment of Educational Progress, 1963-1973.* Unpublished doctoral dissertation, University of Kansas.

Howley, C. (1994). *The academic effectiveness of small-scale schooling.* Charleston, WV: ERIC Clearinghouse on Rural Education and Small Schools. (ERIC Document Reproduction Service No. ED 372 897)

Howley, C. (1996). *Ongoing dilemmas of school size: A short story.* Charleston, WV: ERIC Clearinghouse on Rural Education and Small Schools. (ERIC Document Reproduction Service No. ED 401 089)

Husen, T. (Ed.). (1967). *International study of achievement in mathematics* (Vols. 1 and 2). New York: John Wiley.

Jaeger, R. M., Mullis, I., Bourque, M. L., & Shakrani, S. (1996). Setting performance standards for performance assessments: Some fundamental issues, current practices and technical dilemmas. In G. Phillips (Ed.), *Technical issues in large-scale performance assessment* (NCES Report No. 96-802; pp. 79-116). Washington, DC: National Center for Education Statistics, U.S. Department of Education, Office of Educational Research and Improvement.

Johnson, E. G., Lazer, S., & O'Sullivan, C. Y. (1997). *NAEP reconfigured: An integrated redesign of the National Assessment of Educational Progress* (CFDA No. 84.902A). Washington, DC: U.S. Department of Education, Office of Educational Research and Improvement.

Johnson, E. G., & Rust, K. F. (1992). Population inferences and variance estimation for NAEP data. *Journal of Educational Statistics, 17*(2), 175-90.

Joint Committee on Standards for Educational Evaluation. (1994). *The program evaluation standards: How to assess evaluations of educational programs.* Thousand Oaks, CA: Sage.

Kendall, J. S., & Marzano, R. J. (1996). *Content knowledge: A compendium of standards and benchmarks from K-12 education.* Aurora, CO: Mid-Continent Regional Educational Laboratory

Kifer, E. (1984, July). *Issues and implications of differentiated curriculum in the eighth grade.* Paper delivered at the Atherton Conference, National Conference on Teaching and Learning of Mathematics in the United States, Monticello, IL.

Kifer, E. (1989). What IEA studies say about curriculum and school organization. In A. Purves (Ed.), *International comparisons and educational reform* (pp. 51-72). Alexandria, VA: Association for Supervision and Curriculum Development.

Kifer, E. (1994). Opportunities, talents and participation. In L. Burstein (Ed.), *The IEA study of mathematics III: Student growth and classroom processes* (pp. 279-397). New York: Pergamon.

Koretz, D. M. (1989). The new national assessment: What it can and cannot do. *NEA Today, 7*(6), 32-37.

Koretz, D. M. (1991). State comparisons using NAEP: Large costs, disappointing benefits. *Educational Researcher, 20*(3), 19-21.

Koretz, D. M. (1996). Using student assessments for educational accountability. In E. A. Hanushek & D. W. Jorgenson (Eds.), *Improving America's schools: The role of incentives* (pp. 131-157). Washington, DC: National Academy Press.

Koretz, D. M., Barron, S., Mitchell, K., & Stecher, B. (1996, May). *Perceived effects of the Kentucky Instructional Results Information System (KIRIS).* Santa Monica, CA: RAND.

Koretz, D. M., Mitchell, K., Barron, S., & Keith, S. (1996). *Final report: Perceived effects of the Maryland school performance assessment program* (CSE Technical Report No. 409). Los Angeles: University of California at Los Angeles, Center for Research on Evaluation, Standards, and Student Testing.

Lee, V. E., & Smith, J. B. (1997). High school size: Which works best and for whom? *Educational Evaluation and Policy Analysis, 19*(3), 205-227.

Lewis, G. E., & Massad, C. E. (1975). *The teaching of English as a foreign language in ten countries.* New York: John Wiley.

Linn, R. L. (1998a). *Standards-based accountability: Ten suggestions.* Los Angeles: University of California at Los Angeles, Center for Research on Evaluation, Standards, and Student Testing.

Linn, R. L. (1998b, April). *Assessments and accountability.* Paper presented at the annual meeting of the American Educational Research Association, San Diego, CA.

Linn, R. L., & Baker, E. L. (1999). *Absolutes, wishful thinking, and norms: The CRESST line.* Los Angeles: University of California at Los Angeles, Center for Research on Evaluation, Standards, and Student Testing.

Linn, R. L., & Herman, J. L. (1997). *A policymaker's guide to standards-led assessment* (CSE Technical Report No. 426). Los Angeles: University of California at Los Angeles, Center for Research on Evaluation, Standards, and Student Testing.

Madeus, G. F., & O'Dwyer, L. M. (1999). A short history of performance assessment. *Phi Delta Kappan, 80*(9), 688-695.

Martin, M. O., Mullis, I. V. S., Beaton, A. E., Gonzalez, E. J., Smith, T. A., & Kelly, D. L. (1997). *Science achievement in the primary school years: IEA's Third International Mathematics and Science Study (TIMSS)*. Washington, DC: U.S. Department of Education, Office of Educational Research and Improvement.

Marzano, R. J., & Kendall, J. S. (1996). *Designing standards-based districts, schools, and classrooms*. Alexandria, VA: Association for Supervision and Curriculum Development.

McKnight, C., Crosswhite, F. J., Dossey, J. A., Kifer, E., Swafford, J. O., Travers, K. J., & Cooney, T. J. (1987). *The underachieving curriculum*. Champaign, IL: Stipes.

Meier, D. W. (1995a). *The power of their ideas: Lessons for America from a small school in Harlem*. Boston: Beacon.

Meier, D. W. (1995b). Small schools, big results. *The American School Board Journal, 182*(7), 37-40.

Messick, S., Beaton, A. E., & Lord, F. (1983). *National assessment of educational progress reconsidered: A new design for a new era* (NAEP Report No. 83-1). Princeton, NJ: National Assessment of Educational Progress.

Miller, M. D., & Linn, R. L. (1985). *Cross-national achievement with differential retention rates*. Urbana, IL: University of Illinois Press.

Millman, J. (Ed.). (1997). *Grading teachers, grading schools: Is student achievement a valid evaluation measure?* Thousand Oaks, CA: Corwin.

Mislevy, R. J. (1993). Should "multiple imputations" be treated as "multiple indicators"? *Psychometrika, 58*(1), 79-85.

Mislevy, R. J., Beaton, A. E., Kaplan, B., & Sheehan, K. M. (1992a). Estimating population characteristics from sparse matrix samples of item responses. *Journal of Educational Measurement, 29*(2), 133-161.

Mislevy, R. J., Beaton, A. E., Kaplan, B., & Sheehan, K. M. (1992b). Scaling procedures in NAEP. *Journal of Educational Statistics, 17*(2), 131-154.

Mosteller, F. (1995). The Tennessee study of class size in the early school grades. *Future of Children, 5*(2), 113-127.

Mullis, I.V.S. (1992). Developing the NAEP content-area frameworks and innovative assessment methods in the 1992 assessments of mathematics, reading, and writing. *Journal of Educational Measurement, 29*(2), 111-131.

Muraki, E. (1992). A generalized partial credit model: Application of an EM algorithm. *Applied Psychological Measurement, 16*(2), 159-176.

Muraki, E. (1993). Information functions of the generalized partial credit model. *Applied Psychological Measurement, 17*(4), 351-363.

Musick, M. D. (1997). *Accountability in the 1990s: Holding schools responsible for student achievement*. Atlanta, GA: Southern Regional Accreditation Board.

Musick, M. D. (1998). *Setting education standards high enough*. Atlanta, GA: Southern Regional Education Board.

National Academy of Education. (1993). *Setting performance standards for student achievement. A report of the National Academy of Education Panel on the evaluation of the NAEP trial state assessment: An evaluation of the 1992 achievement levels*. Stanford, CA: Author.

National Assessment Governing Board (NAGB). (1993a). *U.S. history framework for the 1994 National Assessment of Educational Progress*. Washington, DC: Government Printing Office.

National Assessment Governing Board (NAGB). (1993b). *Geography framework for the 1994 National Assessment of Educational Progress*. Washington, DC: Government Printing Office.

National Assessment Governing Board (NAGB). (1995a). *Mathematics framework for the 1996 National Assessment of Educational Progress*. Washington, DC: Government Printing Office.

National Assessment Governing Board (NAGB). (1995b). *Science framework for the 1996 National Assessment of Educational Progress*. Washington, DC: Government Printing Office.

National Center for Education Statistics. (1997). *Video examples from the TIMSS videotape classroom study: Eighth grade mathematics in Germany, Japan, and the United States* [CD-ROM]. (Available from National Center for Education Statistics, Office of Educational Research and Improvement, U.S. Department of Education, 555 New Jersey Avenue N.W., Washington, DC 20208-5574)

National Commission on Excellence in Education. (1983). *A nation at risk: The imperative for educational reform*. Washington, DC: Government Printing Office.

National Council on the Teaching of Mathematics (NCTM). (1989). *Curriculum and evaluation standards for school mathematics*. Reston, VA: Author.

National Council on the Teaching of Mathematics (NCTM). (1995). *Assessment standards for school mathematics*. Reston, VA: Author.

National Goals Panel. (1998). *Promising practices: Progress toward the goals*. Washington, DC: Author.

National Goals Panel. (1999). *Promising practices: Progress toward the goals*. Washington, DC: Author.

Nye, B. A., et al. (1992a, April). *Five years of small-class research: Student benefits derived from reduced student/teacher ratios: Lasting benefits study class-size update for educational practitioners and researchers*. Paper presented at the Annual Meeting of the American Educational Research Association, San Francisco, CA.

Nye, B. A., et al. (1992b). *The lasting benefits study. A continuing analysis of the effect of small class size in kindergarten through third grade on student achievement test scores in subsequent grade levels: Fifth grade.* Nashville: Tennessee State University, Center of Excellence.

Pelgrum, W. J., & Plomp, T. (1993). *The IEA study of computers in education: Implementation of an innovation in 21 education systems* (1st ed.). Oxford, UK: Pergamon.

Pellegrino, J. W., Jones, L. R., & Mitchell, K. J. (1998). *Grading the nation's report card.* Washington, DC: National Academy Press.

Phillips, G. W. (1991). Benefits of state-by-state comparisons. *Educational Researcher, 20*(3), 17-19.

Phillips, G. W. (Ed.). (1996). *Technical issues in large-scale performance assessment* (NCES Report No. 96-802). Washington, DC: National Center for Education Statistics, U.S. Department of Education, Office of Educational Research and Improvement.

Porter, A. C. (1995). The uses and misuses of opportunity-to-learn standards. *Educational Researcher, 24*(1), 21-27.

Purves, A. (1973). *Literature education in ten countries.* New York: John Wiley.

Purves, A. (Ed.). (1989). *International comparisons and educational reform.* Alexandria, VA: Association for Supervision and Curriculum Development.

Rapple, B. A. (1994). Payment by results: An example of assessment in elementary education from nineteenth century Britain. *Education Policy Analysis Archives, 2,* 1.

Raywid, M. A. (1996). *Taking stock: The movement to create mini-schools, schools-within-schools, and separate small schools.* Madison, WI: Center on Organization and Restructuring of Schools. (ERIC Document Reproduction Service No. ED 393 958)

Resnick, L. B., et al. (1995). Benchmarking education standards. *Educational Evaluation and Policy Analysis, 17*(4), 438-461.

Resnick, L. B., & Resnick D. P. (1992). Assessing the thinking curriculum: New tools for educational reform. In B. R. Gifford & M. C. O'Connor (Eds.), *Changing assessments: Alternative views of aptitude, achievement and instruction* (pp. 271-312). Boston: Kluwer.

Robitaille, D. (Ed.). (1993). *Curriculum frameworks for mathematics and science. The Third International Mathematics and Science Study* (TIMSS Monograph No. 1). Vancouver, Canada: Pacific Education.

Rose v Council for Better Education, Inc., KY 88-SC-804-TG (September 28, 1989).

Russell, M. (1998). Testing on computers: A follow-up study comparing performance on computer and on paper. *Educational Policy Analysis Archives, 7,* 20.

Russell, M., & Haney, W. (1997). Testing writing on computers: An experiment comparing student performance on tests conducted via computer and via paper-and-pencil. *Educational Policy Analysis Archives, 5,* 3.

Rutter, R. A. (1988). *Effects of school as a community.* Madison, WI: National Center on Effective Secondary Schools. (ERIC Document Reproduction Service No. ED 313 470)

Sanders, W. (1998). Value-added assessment. *The School Administrator, 55*(11), 35-47.

Sanders, W., Saxton, A., & Horn, S. (1997). The Tennessee value-added assessment system: A quantitative, outcomes-based approach to educational assessment. In J. Millman (Ed.), *Grading teachers, grading schools* (pp. 137-162). Thousand Oaks, CA: Corwin.

Schmidt, W. H., McKnight, C. C., Cogan, L. S., Jakwerth, P. M., & Houang, R. T. (1999). *Facing the consequences: Using TIMSS for a closer look at U.S. mathematics and science.* Boston: Kluwer.

Schmidt, W. H., McKnight, C. C., & Raizen, S. (1997). *A splintered vision: An investigation of U.S. science and mathematics education.* Dordrecht, the Netherlands: Kluwer.

Scriven, M. (1967). The methodology of evaluation. In R. Tyler, R. M. Gagne, & M. Scriven (Eds.), *Perspectives of curriculum evaluation* (AERA Monograph Series on Curriculum Evaluation, No. 1). Chicago: Rand McNally.

Silver, E. A., & Kenney, P. A. (1993). An examination of relationships between the 1990 NAEP mathematics items for Grade 8 and selected themes from the NCTM standards. *Journal for Research in Mathematics Education, 24*(2), 159-167.

Smith, M. S., O'Day, J., & Fuhrman, S. H. (1992). State policy and systemic school reform. *Educational Technology, 32*(11), 31-36.

Stake, R. (1999). The goods on American education. *Phi Delta Kappan, 80*(9), 668-672.

Stiefel, L., Iatarola, P., Fruchter, N., & Berne, R. (1998). *The effects of size of student body on school costs and performance in New York City high schools.* New York: New York University, Institute for Education and Social Policy.

Stufflebeam, D. L., Jaeger, R. M., & Scriven, M. (1991). *Summative evaluation of the National Assessment Governing Board's inaugural 1990-1991 effort to set achievement levels on the National Assessment of Educational Progress.* Washington, DC: National Assessment Governing Board.

Thomas B. Fordham Foundation. (1998). *A nation still at risk: An education manifesto.* Washington, DC: Author.

Thorndike, R. L. (1973). *Reading comprehension education in fourteen countries: An empirical study.* New York: John Wiley.

Torney, J. V., Oppenheim, A. N., & Farnen, P. E. (1975). *Civics education in ten countries.* New York: John Wiley.

Trimble, C. S. (1994). Ensuring educational accountability. In T. Guskey (Ed.), *High stakes performance assessment: Perspectives on Kentucky's educational reform* (pp. 37-54). Thousand Oaks, CA: Corwin.

Tyler, R. (1949). *Basic principles of curriculum and instruction.* Chicago: University of Chicago Press.

Tyler, R. (1970). National assessment: A history and sociology. *School and Society, 96,* 23-29.

U.S. Department of Education. (1998a). *Eighth-grade findings from the National Assessment of Educational Progress* (NCES Report No. 1999-485). Washington, DC: Author.

U.S. Department of Education. (1998b). *Pursuing excellence: A study of U.S. twelfth-grade mathematics and science achievement in international context* (NCES Report No. 998-049). Washington, DC: Author.

Vitali, G. J. (1993). *Factors influencing teachers' assessment and instructional practices in an assessment driven educational reform.* Unpublished doctoral dissertation, University of Kentucky.

Westbury, I. (1989). The problems of comparing curriculums across educational systems. In A. Purves (Ed.), *International comparisons and educational reform* (pp. 17-34). Alexandria, VA: Association for Supervision and Curriculum Development.

Westbury, I. (1992). Comparing American and Japanese achievement: Is the United States really a low achiever? *Educational Researcher, 21*(5), 18-24.

Williams, P. L., Lazer, S., Reese, C. M. (1995). *NAEP 1994 U.S. history: A first look.* Washington, DC: U.S. Department of Education, Office of Educational Research and Improvement.

Wolf, R. M. (1992). What can we learn from state NAEP? *Educational Measurement: Issues and Practice, 11*(4), 12-18.

Zorn, J. (1994). The NAEP 1992 reading report card: Useless-and-worse psychometry. *English Journal, 63*(4), 38-39.

Zwick, R. (1992). Statistical and psychometric issues in the measurement of educational achievement trends: Examples from the National Assessment of Educational Progress. *Journal of Educational Statistics, 17*(2), 205-218.

Index